Python Crash Course

The Perfect Beginner's Guide to Learning Programming with Python on a Crash Course Even If You're New to Programming

By

Aiden Phillips

PYTHON

A Highly Expressive
Programming Language..

Table of Contents

PYTHON FOR BEGINNERS

PYTHON PROGRAMMING

Python for Beginners

A complete beginner's guide to learning Python with a programming-based introduction and a hands-on computer coding exercise

By

Aiden Phillips

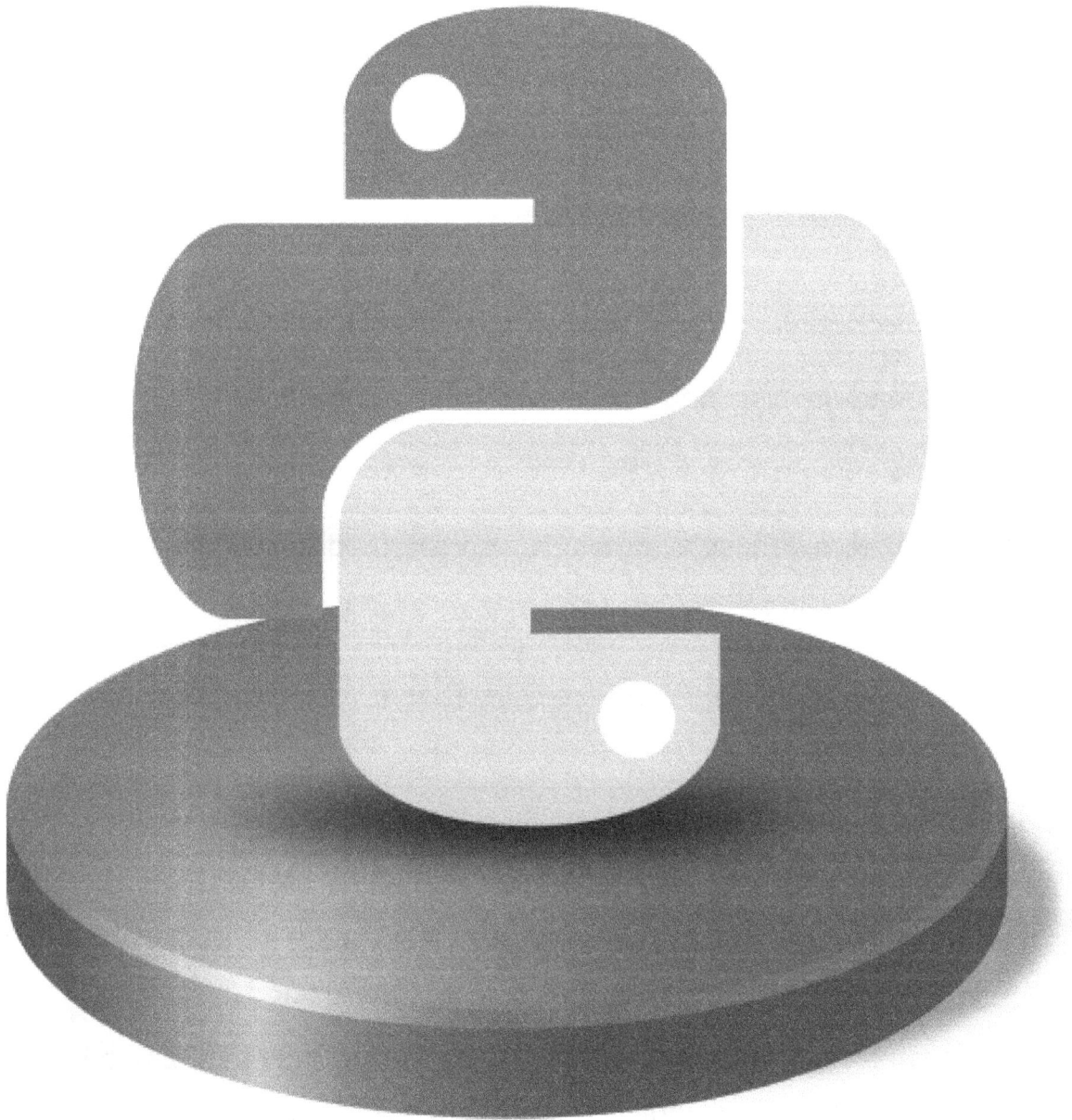

Introduction:

Python is a famous programming language. It was developed by Guido van and launched in 1991.

It can be used for:

- Server-side web development

- Software development

- Mathematics

- System scripting

Python is used to develop web applications on a server.

Python is used along with software that creates workflows.

Python can link to database systems. It also can modify and read files.

Python is used to hold large data and execute complex mathematics.

Python is used for production-ready software development and rapid prototyping.

Python runs on various systems (Mac, Windows, Raspberry Pi, Linux, etc.). Python has a plain syntax close to English. Python has a syntax that enables developers to compose programs with fewer lines than any other programming language.

Python operates on an interpreter machine, ensuring the code may be run as quickly as it is written. This indicates that prototyping might be easy. Python may be handled in a sequential manner, logical way, or object-oriented way.

The most current big edition of Python is Version 3. However, Python 2, while not being modified with anything except security fixes, is still very common.

Python can be written inside of an (IDE) Integrated Development Environment, such as Thonny, Pycharm, Netbeans, or Eclipse, which is especially helpful when working with vast sets of Python data. By comparing Python syntax to those of other programming languages, Python was created with readability in mind, and it bears a certain resemblance to the English language, with a mathematical effect.

In contrast to other programming languages, Python uses fresh lines to complete commands, rather than semicolons or parentheses. Indentation and whitespace are used in Python to describe the scope, as the range of loops, functions, and groups. Curly brackets are often used in other programming languages for this reason.

Python is a scripting language that can lead to a broad range of well-paying careers in several areas, such as computer science and web creation.

It is reasonably simple to learn as opposed to almost every other programming language and, in most cases; Python has fewer lines of code than most programming languages.

Python is a high-purpose language of programming that is gaining in popularity as a data science programming language. Python is being used by businesses all over the world to extract information from their data to achieve a strategic advantage.

Learning Python opens up a vast range of job options for programmers. Python is a free and open-source programming language used in software development, computer science, AI, and a variety of research applications.

Learning Python encourages a programmer to concentrate on problem-solving rather than syntax. Its small size and simple syntax offer it an advantage over languages like C++ and Java, but the availability of libraries gives it the ability to do amazing stuff.

Chapter 1: Variables and Operators

1.1Variables:

Variables are storage bins for values of data. The only reserved memory places where values can be stored are variables. This implies that anytime you make the variable, we set aside any memory for it. An interpreter allots resources and specifies what should be placed in a memory that is allocated based on the data form of a variable. As a result, you can store numbers, characters or decimals by allocating different types of data to them in variables.

Creating a variable:

Declaring a variable in Python is not possible directly via command. When you first allocate a value to a variable, it is said to be formed. The variables do not have to be assigned for a certain category, and they may also modify types after being set.

```
x = 3
y = "Ali"
print(x)
print(y)
```

```
3
Ali
```

Variable casting:

Casting may be used to define the type of data of a variable.

```
x = str(7)
y = int(7)
z = float(7)

print(x)
print(y)
print(z)
```

```
7
7
7.0
```

Get the type:

The type() method returns the type of data of a variable.

```
x = 2
y = "Ali"
print(type(x))
print(type(y))
```

```
<class 'int'>
<class 'str'>
```

Single or Double Quotes?

Single and double quotes may be used to declare string variables.

```
x = "Ali"
print(x)
#double quotes are the same as single quotes:
x = 'Ali'
print(x)
```

```
Ali
Ali
```

Case-Sensitive:

Names of the variables are case-sensitive.

```
a = 5
A = "Anaya"

print(a)
print(A)
```

```
5
Anaya
```

1.1.1 Variables Names:

A variable may have a concise name such as x and y or even a longer name such as class, book_name, or total_inches.

Rules for Python variables:

The name of a variable must begin with the underscore character or with a letter.

A number cannot be the first character in a variable name.

Only underscore (A-z, _, 0-9) and alphanumeric characters are used in variable names.

Case matters when it comes to variable titles i.e. name, Name, and NAME are three separate variables.

Multi Words Variable Names:

It may be challenging to interpret variable names that include more than one word.

You may use a variety of methods to have them easy to read:

Camel case:

Except for the first, each term begins with a capital letter.

myVariableName = "Ali"

Pascal case:

The first letter of each word is capitalized.

MyVariableName = "Ali"

Snake case:

An underscore character separates each word.

my_variable_name = "Ali"

1.1.2   Assign multiple values:

Many Variables with a Wide Range of Values:

You can allocate values to several variables in a single line in Python.

Many variables with a single value:

You may also use a single line to apply the same meaning to different variables.

```
x = y = z = "Shirt"

print(x)
print(y)
print(z)
```

```
Shirt
Shirt
Shirt
```

Organize/Unpack a Collection:

If you have a number, tuple, or another set of values, you may use this method. Python helps you to remove values and store them in variables. This is referred to as unpacking.

```python
fruits = ["grapes", "orange", "strawberry"]
x, y, z = fruits

print(x)
print(y)
print(z)
```

```
grapes
orange
strawberry
```

1.1.3   Output variables:

The print expression in Python is sometimes used to output values.

The + character is used to merge text and a variable.

You may also bind a variable to the next variable by using the + symbol.

The + character serves as a logical operator for numbers. Python can throw an error if you attempt to merge numbers and strings.

1.1.4   Variables at a Global Level:

Global variables are variables that are generated outside of a function.

All should use global variables, both within and outside of functions.

If you construct a variable of the same name within a feature, it would be local, meaning it can only be found inside that function. The global variable of the same name would stay global and have the same meaning as before.

```python
x = "lovely"

def myfunc():
  x = "awesome"
  print("Weather is " + x)

myfunc()

print("Weather is " + x)
```

```
Weather is awesome
Weather is lovely
```

The global keywords:

When you generate a variable within a feature, it is usually local, meaning it can only be found inside that function.

The global keyword may be used to construct a global variable within a function.

If you want to modify a global variable within a function, use the global keyword.

1.2 Operators:

Variables and values are operated on with the help of operators.

Python categorizes the operators into the following categories:

- Arithmetic operators

- Assignment operators

- Logical operators

- Identity operators

- Comparison operators

- Bitwise operators

- Membership operators

Arithmetic operators:

To conduct basic mathematical operations, arithmetic operators are required with numeric values.

Operator	Meaning	Example
+	Add two operands or unary plus	x + y+ 2
-	Subtract right operand from the left or unary minus	x - y- 2
*	Multiply two operands	x * y
/	Divide left operand by the right one (always results into float)	x / y
%	Modulus - remainder of the division of left operand by the right	x % y (remainder of x/y)
//	Floor division - division that results into whole number adjusted to the left in the number line	x // y
**	Exponent - left operand raised to the power of right	x**y (x to the power y)

Assignment operators:

To allocate values to variables, assignment operators are used.

Operator	Example	Equivalent to
=	x = 5	x = 5
+=	x += 5	x = x + 5
-=	x -= 5	x = x - 5
*=	x *= 5	x = x * 5
/=	x /= 5	x = x / 5
%=	x %= 5	x = x % 5
//=	x //= 5	x = x // 5
**=	x **= 5	x = x ** 5
&=	x &= 5	x = x & 5
|=	x |= 5	x = x | 5
^=	x ^= 5	x = x ^ 5
>>=	x >>= 5	x = x >> 5
<<=	x <<= 5	x = x << 5

Logical operators:

To merge conditional statements, logical operators are used.

Operator	Meaning	Example
and	True if both the operands are true	x and y
or	True if either of the operands is true	x or y
not	True if operand is false (complements the operand)	not x

Identity operators:

Identity operators are required to evaluate objects to see if they are the same object, with the exact memory location, rather than if they are equal.

Operator	Meaning	Example
is	True if the operands are identical (refer to the same object)	x is True
is not	True if the operands are not identical (do not refer to the same object)	x is not True

Comparison operators:

To equate two values, comparison operators are used.

Operator	Meaning	Example
>	Greater than - True if left operand is greater than the right	x > y
<	Less than - True if left operand is less than the right	x < y
==	Equal to - True if both operands are equal	x == y
!=	Not equal to - True if operands are not equal	x != y
>=	Greater than or equal to - True if left operand is greater than or equal to the right	x >= y
<=	Less than or equal to - True if left operand is less than or equal to the right	x <= y

Bitwise operators:

For comparing binary numbers, bitwise operators are used.

Operator	Meaning	Example
&	Bitwise AND	x & y = 0 (0000 0000)
|	Bitwise OR	x | y = 14 (0000 1110)
~	Bitwise NOT	~x = -11 (1111 0101)
^	Bitwise XOR	x ^ y = 14 (0000 1110)
>>	Bitwise right shift	x >> 2 = 2 (0000 0010)
<<	Bitwise left shift	x << 2 = 40 (0010 1000)

Membership operators:

To see whether a series is present in an entity, we use the membership operators.

Operator	Meaning	Example
in	True if value/variable is found in the sequence	5 in x
not in	True if value/variable is not found in the sequence	5 not in x

Chapter 2: Datatypes

The data type is a crucial term in programming. Variables can hold a variety of data, and various types can perform different tasks. In Python, each value has a datatype. Data types are simply groups, and variables are instances (objects) of these classes, so anything in Python programming is an entity.

2.1 Built-in datatypes:

Python has many different data formats. Python consists of the below data types pre-installed in these categories:

Text Type:	str
Numeric Types:	int, float, complex
Sequence Types:	list, tuple, range
Mapping Type:	dict
Set Types:	set, frozenset
Boolean Type:	bool
Binary Types:	bytes, bytearray, memoryview

Setting the Data Type:

When you allocate a value to a variable, the data type is set in python.

```
x = "Hi, I am Ali"

#display x:
print(x)

#display the data type of x:
print(type(x))
```

```
Hi, I am Ali
<class 'str'>
```

Getting the datatype:

The type() method may be used to determine the type of data of any object.

```
x = 7
print(type(x))
```

```
<class 'int'>
```

Setting a particular datatype:

The constructor functions mentioned below may be used to define the data type.

```
x = bool(2)

#display x:
print(x)

#display the data type of x:
print(type(x))
```

```
True
<class 'bool'>
```

Chapter 3: Data Structures

Data organization, management, and storage are critical since they allow for faster access and more reliable changes. Data Structures help you to arrange the data in a manner that allows you to store sets of data, link them together and execute operations on them.

Python Data structures:

Data Structures are built-in to Python and allow you to save and view data. List, Dictionary, Tuple, and Set are the names of these constructs. Users may build their specific Data Structures in Python, giving them complete power of their features. The most common Data Structures include Stack, Queue, Tree, and Linked List, which are also accessible in many other programming languages.

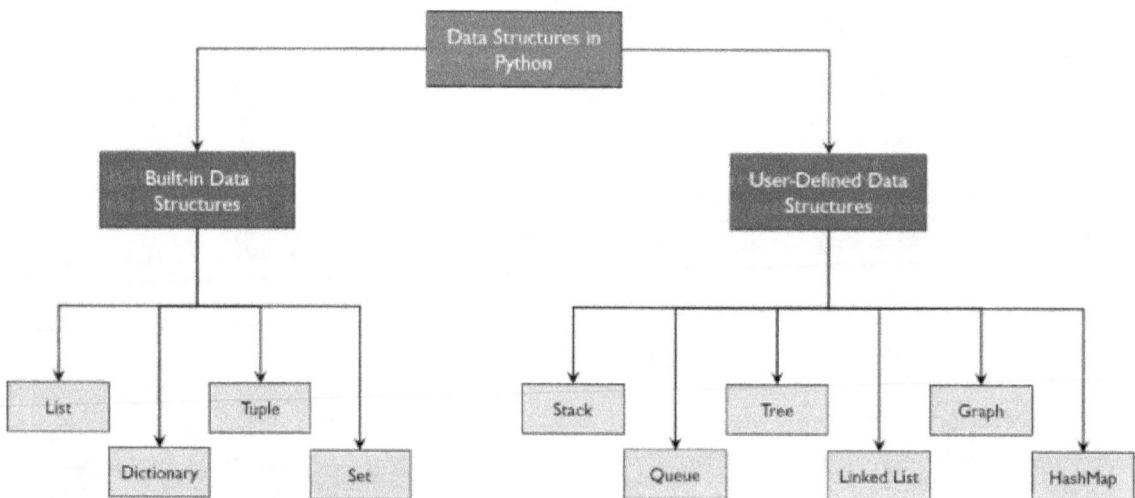

3.1   Built-in data structures:

The data structures are built-in with Python, as the name implies, making programming simpler and allowing programmers to obtain solutions quicker. Let's take a closer look at each of them.

3.1.1 Lists:

Lists are required to hold data of various kinds in a logical order. Any member of the list has an address, which is referred to as the Index. The index value begins at 0 and continues until the last variable, which is referred to as the positive index. Negative indexing, which begins at -1, allows you to view items from last to the first.

List Creation:

You use square brackets to make a list and then add elements to it if required. If no elements are passed within the square brackets, the output is an empty set.

```
my_list = [] #create empty list
print(my_list)
my_list = [6, 7, 8, 'people', 5.455] #creating list with data
print(my_list)
```

```
[]
[6, 7, 8, 'people', 5.455]
```

Elements Addition:

- The append(), extend(), and insert() functions may be used to add elements to the list.

- The append() function combines all of the elements transferred to it into one.

- The extend() function adds each element to the list one by one.

- The insert() function increases the list's size by adding the element moved to the index value.

```
my_list = [3, 4, 5]
print(my_list)
my_list.append([333, 17]) #add as a single element
print(my_list)
my_list.extend([567, 'data_sample']) #add as different elements
print(my_list)
my_list.insert(8, 'insert_data') #add element i
print(my_list)
```

```
[3, 4, 5]
[3, 4, 5, [333, 17]]
[3, 4, 5, [333, 17], 567, 'data_sample']
[3, 4, 5, [333, 17], 567, 'data_sample', 'insert_data']
```

Deleting the Elements:

- The del keyword is built-in to Python and can be used to delete elements, but it does not return anything.

- You use the pop() method, which uses the index value, to get the element back.

- The remove() method is used to extract an element based on its significance.

```python
my_list = [4, 7, 3, 'book', 6.987, 12, 84]
del my_list[5] #delete element at index 5
print(my_list)
my_list.remove('book') #remove element with value
print(my_list)
a = my_list.pop(1) #pop element from list
print('Popped Element: ', a, ' List remaining: ', my_list)
my_list.clear() #empty the list
print(my_list)
```

```
[4, 7, 3, 'book', 6.987, 84]
[4, 7, 3, 6.987, 84]
Popped Element:  7  List remaining:  [4, 3, 6.987, 84]
[]
```

Accessing the Elements:

In Python, accessing elements is much like accessing Strings. You can acquire the values as desired bypassing the index values.

```python
my_list = [5, 6, 7, 'book', 5.876, 15, 78]
for element in my_list: #access elements one by one
    print(element)
print(my_list) #access all elements
print(my_list[3]) #access index 3 element
print(my_list[0:2]) #access elements from 0 to 1 and exclude 2
print(my_list[::-1]) #access elements in reverse
```

```
5
6
7
book
5.876
15
78
[5, 6, 7, 'book', 5.876, 15, 78]
book
[5, 6]
[78, 15, 5.876, 'book', 7, 6, 5]
```

Other Functions:

When dealing with lists, you may use a variety of other features.

- The length of a list is returned by the len() method.

- The index() method returns an index value of the transferred value where it was first encountered.

- The count() function returns the number of times the value transferred to it has been counted.

27

- A sort() and sorted() functions both do the same thing: they sort the list's values. The sorted() function returns a value, while the sort() function modifies the initial array.

```python
my_list = [8, 4, 2, 65, 24, 17]
print(len(my_list)) #find length of list
print(my_list.index(17)) #find index of element that occurs first
print(my_list.count(17)) #find count of the element
print(sorted(my_list)) #print sorted list but not change original
my_list.sort(reverse=True) #sort original list
print(my_list)
```

```
6
5
1
[2, 4, 8, 17, 24, 65]
[65, 24, 17, 8, 4, 2]
```

3.1.2 Dictionary:

Key-value pairs are stored in dictionaries. Consider a phone book of hundreds of thousands of names and its accompanying phone numbers. Name and Phone Numbers are the constant values here, and they are referred to as the buttons. The values which have been fed to the keys are different names and phone numbers. You will get all phone numbers and names if you look at the key values. That is the definition of a key-value pair. Dictionaries are used to store this framework in Python.

Dictionary Creation:

The dict() function or the flower braces may be used to construct dictionaries. When working with dictionaries, you must still include the key-value pairs.

```python
my_dict = {} #empty dictionary
print(my_dict)
my_dict = {1: 'program', 2: 'exercise'} #dictionary with elements
print(my_dict)
```

```
{}
{1: 'program', 2: 'exercise'}
```

Adding and Changing key, value pairs:

You must use the keys to adjust the dictionary's values. As a result, you must first access the key before changing the value. Consider adding other key-value pairs as shown here to add values.

```python
my_dict = {'First': 'Book', 'Second': 'Notebook'}
print(my_dict)
my_dict['Second'] = 'Pencil' #changing element
print(my_dict)
my_dict['Third'] = 'Ruler' #adding key-value pair
```

```
{'First': 'Book', 'Second': 'Notebook'}
{'First': 'Book', 'Second': 'Pencil'}
```

Key, value pairs Deletion:

- Use the pop() method to delete the values, which yields the value which has been removed.

- Use the popitem() method to get the key-value pair, which yields a tuple with the key and value.

- The clear() method is used to clear the whole dictionary.

```
my_dict = {'First': 'Notebook', 'Second': 'Book', 'Third': 'Pen'}
a = my_dict.pop('Third') #pop element
print('Value:', a)
print('Dictionary:', my_dict)
b = my_dict.popitem() #pop the key-value pair
print('Key, value pair:', b)
print('Dictionary', my_dict)
my_dict.clear() #empty dictionary
print('n', my_dict)
```

```
Value: Pen
Dictionary: {'First': 'Notebook', 'Second': 'Book'}
Key, value pair: ('Second', 'Book')
Dictionary {'First': 'Notebook'}
n {}
```

Accessing the Elements:

Just the keys may be used to unlock elements. You may use the get() method or simply transfer the main values and the values would be returned.

```
my_dict = {'First': 'Pen', 'Second': 'Notebook'}
print(my_dict['First']) #access elements using keys
print(my_dict.get('Second'))
```

```
Pen
Notebook
```

Other Functions:

You have various functions that return the keys or value of key-value pair under the keys(), values(), and items() functions.

```
my_dict = {'First': 'Book', 'Second': 'Pen', 'Third': 'Ruler'}
print(my_dict.keys()) #get keys
print(my_dict.values()) #get values
print(my_dict.items()) #get key-value pairs
print(my_dict.get('First'))
```

```
dict_keys(['First', 'Second', 'Third'])
dict_values(['Book', 'Pen', 'Ruler'])
dict_items([('First', 'Book'), ('Second', 'Pen'), ('Third', 'Ruler')])
Book
```

3.1.3 Tuples:

Tuples are similar to lists, along with the exception that once data is inserted into a tuple, it cannot be modified. And where the data inside of the tuple is mutable will the tuple data be modified. The sample software can aid in your comprehension.

Tuple Creation:

Using parenthesis or the tuple() function, you can make a tuple.

```
my_tuple = (5, 6, 7) #create tuple
print(my_tuple)
```

```
(5, 6, 7)
```

Accessing the Elements:

Accessing elements in a collection is the same as accessing attributes in a list.

```
my_tuple2 = (7, 8, 9, 'paprika') #access elements
for x in my_tuple2:
    print(x)
print(my_tuple2)
print(my_tuple2[0])
print(my_tuple2[:])
print(my_tuple2[3][4])
```

```
7
8
9
paprika
(7, 8, 9, 'paprika')
7
(7, 8, 9, 'paprika')
i
```

Appending the Elements:

To append the elements, you use the '+' operator, which accepts another tuple as input.

```
my_tuple = (6, 7, 8)
my_tuple = my_tuple + (2, 3, 4) #add elements
print(my_tuple)
```

```
(6, 7, 8, 2, 3, 4)
```

Other Functions:

These functions are identical to those used in lists.

```
my_tuple = (1, 2, 3, ['urdu', 'program'])
my_tuple[3][0] = 'punjabi'
print(my_tuple)
print(my_tuple.count(2))
print(my_tuple.index(['punjabi', 'program']))
```

```
(1, 2, 3, ['punjabi', 'program'])
1
3
```

3.1.4 Sets:

Sets are a set of special, unordered elements. That is, even though the data is replicated several times, it would only be inserted into the set once. It's similar to the sets you've seen in algebra. As with the arithmetic sets, the procedures are all the same.

Set Creation:

The flower braces are used to build sets, but instead of inserting key-value pairs, you simply transfer values to them.

```
my_set = {5, 6, 7, 8, 9, 9, 9} #create set
print(my_set)
```

```
{5, 6, 7, 8, 9}
```

Adding the Elements:

The add() function is used to add elements, and the value is passed to it.

```
my_set = {4, 5, 6}
my_set.add(7) #add element to set
print(my_set)
```

```
{4, 5, 6, 7}
```

Operations in Sets:

Below are examples of fixed operations such as union, intersection, and so on.

```
my_set = {1, 2, 3, 4}
my_set_2 = {3, 4, 5, 6}
print(my_set.union(my_set_2), '----------', my_set | my_set_2)
print(my_set.intersection(my_set_2), '----------', my_set & my_set_2)
print(my_set.difference(my_set_2), '----------', my_set - my_set_2)
print(my_set.symmetric_difference(my_set_2), '----------', my_set ^ my_set_2)
my_set.clear()
print(my_set)
```

```
{1, 2, 3, 4, 5, 6} ---------- {1, 2, 3, 4, 5, 6}
{3, 4} ---------- {3, 4}
{1, 2} ---------- {1, 2}
{1, 2, 5, 6} ---------- {1, 2, 5, 6}
set()
```

- The union() method joins the data from both sets respectively.

- The intersection() method only returns data that is present in both sets.

- The difference() function removes data from both sets and only outputs data from the set transferred.

- The symmetric difference() function is identical to the difference() function, but it outputs the data both from sets.

31

3.2　User-defined Data Structures:

Arrays and Lists:

For one exception, lists and arrays are the same structure. Lists allow for the storing of heterogeneous data elements, while Arrays only allow for the storage of homogeneous elements.

Stack:

Stacks are those linear data structures that work under the Last-In-First-Out (LIFO) model, which means that data reached last is the first to be accessed. It is constructed using an array layout that includes operations such as pressing/adding elements, popping/deleting elements, and only accessing elements from the TOP of the stack. This TOP is a reference to the stack's current location. Recursive programming, reversing sentences, undo methods in word editors, and other programs use stacks extensively.

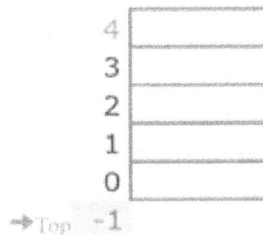

Queue:

A queue is a sequential data structure based on the First-In-First-Out (FIFO) theorem, which states that the data reached first would be processed first. It is constructed using an array structure that includes operations that can be done from both the head and tail edges of the Queue, i.e., front-back and back-to-front. En-Queue and De-Queue operations are used to connect and delete items, and retrieving the elements is possible. Queues are employed as Network Buffers to handle traffic congestion, as well as Job Scheduling in Operating Systems.

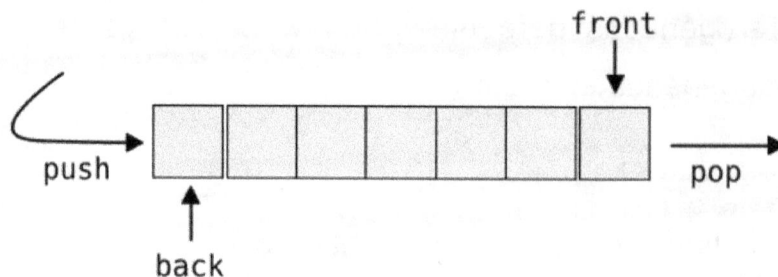

Trees:

Non-linear Data Structures with a base and nodes are known as trees. The root is the point from which the data comes, and the points are the different data points we have access to. The parent is the node that comes before the infant, and the child is the node that comes after it. A tree must have levels to reflect the scope of detail. The leaves are the final nodes in a chain. Trees construct a hierarchy that can be applied in a variety of real-world scenarios, such as identifying which tag belongs to a block in HTML pages. It's also useful for browsing and a variety of other items.

Linked List:

Linked lists are static Data Structures that are linked together using pointers rather than being placed sequentially. A connected list node is made up of a pointer named next and data. These mechanisms are more often found in picture displays, music player, and other applications.

Graph:

Graphs are designed to hold data in the form of vertices/nodes and edges (connections) (edges). The most precise description of a map of the real world can be found in graphs. They are used to pick the least direction by calculating the different cost-to-distance among the diverse data points known as nodes. Many apps, like Uber, Google Maps, and others, use graphs to locate the shortest distance and maximize income in the most efficient way possible.

HashMaps:

In Python, HashMaps are just like dictionaries. They can be used to create apps like phonebooks, populate data based on lists, and many more.

Chapter 4: Input printing and Output formatting

4.1   Input Printing:

Developers are often required to communicate with consumers, either to obtain data or to produce a response. The majority of applications currently use a dialogue box to query the consumer for some kind of feedback. In Python, we have two built-in functions for reading data from the keyboard.

1. input (prompt)

2. raw_input (prompt)

input(prompt):

This feature takes the user's input and then executes the expression, which ensures Python identifies whether the user entered a string, a number, or a list automatically. Python can raise a syntax error or an exception if the information given is incorrect.

Python program showing

use of input()

val = input("Enter your value: ")

print(val)

How the input function works in Python:

When the input() method is called, the software flow is halted before the user provides input.

The text or notification that appears on the output window to encourage the user to insert an input value is discretionary, i.e. the prompt that appears on screen is not needed.

35

The input function converts anything you type into a string. And if an integer value is entered, the input() function converts it to a string. You must use typecasting to directly translate to an integer in the code.

```
# Program to check input

# type in Python

num = input ("Enter number :")

print(num)

name1 = input("Enter name : ")

print(name1)

# Printing type of input value

print ("type of number", type(num))

print ("type of name", type(name1))
```

raw_input(prompt):

This feature is used in older versions of the software (like Python 2.x). This method takes what is entered from the keyboard, converts it to a string, and returns it to the variable we want to store it in.

```
# Python program showing

# use of raw_input()

g = raw_input("Enter your name : ")

print g
```

g is a vector that will receive the string value typed by the user during the program execution. The enter key stops data typing for the raw input() call.

Raw input() may also be used to insert numeric results. In any case, typecasting is used. Refer to this for further details on typecasting.

4.2   Output Formatting:

There are many ways to display a program's output: data may be published in a human-readable format, saved to a disc for later use, or shown in some other manner. Users frequently want greater power over output formatting than just printing space-separated values. There are many options for output formatting.

For using formatted string literals, precede triple quotation mark or the opening quotation mark with f or F.

The str.format() function of strings allows a consumer to make a fancier version of a document. Result

Users may build whatever interface they like by utilizing concatenation operations and string slicing to do all of the string handlings. The string class has a few methods that can be used to pad strings to certain column width.

Output Formatting by String modulo operator(%) :

String formatting may also be done using the percent operator. It perceives the left argument as a printf()-style format to be added to the right argument in C language. While Python does not have a printf() feature, it does have the features of the old printf. The % modulo operator is overloaded by string class to conduct string formatting for this reason. As a result, it's sometimes referred to as a string modulo or even modulus operator.

In Python(3.x), a string modulo operator % is still usable, and it is commonly used. However, the old formatting style is no longer used in the language.

In our case, there are 2 of them: "% 2d" and "% 5.2f." A format placeholder has the following general syntax:

%[flags][width][.precision]type

Let's take a glance at our example's placeholders.

```python
# Python program showing how to use
# string modulo operator(%) to print
# fancier output

# print integer and float value
print("Python : %2d, Portal : %5.2f" % (1, 05.333))

# print integer value
print("Total students : %3d, Boys : %2d" % (240, 120))

# print octal value
print("%7.3o" % (25))

# print exponential value
print("%10.3E" % (356.08977))
```

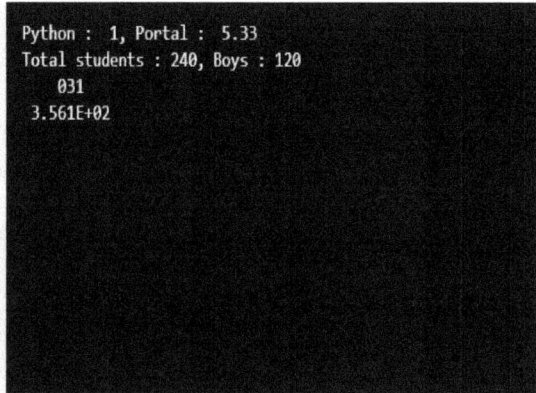

```
Python :  1, Portal :  5.33
Total students : 240, Boys : 120
    031
 3.561E+02
```

The first placeholder, "percent 2d," refers to the first element of our tuple, which is the integer 1. Two characters will be written on the number. The performance is filled with 1 led blanks since 1 is just one digit.

The second one, "percent 5.2f," is a float number type definition. It begins with the percent character, as do other placeholders. The overall amount of digits, the string must comprise is then provided. All digits and decimal points, before the actual decimal point, are included in this figure.

Our float number, 05.333, needs a five-character format. The precision, or decimal component of the integer, is fixed to 2, which is the number after the "." in the placeholder. Finally, the letter "f" stands for "float" in our placeholder.

Output Formatting by the format method:

Python introduced the format() tool (2.6). The string format approach necessitates further manual labor. Users will use to indicate where a variable will be inserted to have specific formatting directives, but they must also supply the data to be formatted. This approach uses positional formatting to concatenate items inside an output.

```
# Python program showing
# a use of format() method

# combining positional and keyword arguments
print('Famous saying is {0}, {1}, {other}.'
    .format('Tit', 'For', other ='Tat'))

# using format() method with number
print("Tit :{0:2d}, Tat :{1:8.2f}".
    format(12, 00.546))

# Changing positional argument
print("Second argument: {1:3d}, first one: {0:7.2f}".
    format(47.42, 11))

print("Tit: {a:5d}, Tat: {p:8.2f}".
    format(a = 453, p = 59.058))
```

```
Famous saying is Tit, For,  Tat.
Tit :12, Tat :    0.55
Second argument:  11, first one:    47.42
Tit:   453, Tat:    59.06
```

Output Formatting by the String method:

Concatenation operations and string slicing are used to format this data. The string sort has several methods for formatting results in a more elegant manner. str.ljust(), str.rjust(), and str.centre() are several of the methods that assist with performance formatting ().

```
# Python program to
# format a output using
# string() method

cstr = "I love Python"

# Printing the center aligned
# string with fillchr
print ("Center aligned string with fillchr: ")
print (cstr.center(40, '#'))

# Printing the left aligned
# string with "-" padding
print ("The left aligned string is : ")
print (cstr.ljust(40, '-'))

# Printing the right aligned string
# with "-" padding
print ("The right aligned string is : ")
print (cstr.rjust(40, '-'))
```

```
Center aligned string with fillchr:
#############I love Python#############
The left aligned string is :
I love Python---------------------------
The right aligned string is :
---------------------------I love Python
```

Chapter 5: Conditional statements and control flow statements

5.1 Conditional Statements:

In Python, based on whether a given Boolean constraint returns to true or false, conditional statements execute various computations or behaviors. In Python, IF statements manage conditional statements.

- If statements in Python manage conditional statements.

- If one of the criteria is valid or incorrect, the "if condition" is used to display out the answer.

- If the one condition ceases to satisfy the criteria, you will use the "else condition" to print the argument.

When you have a third option as a result, you use the "elif scenario." To search for the 4th, 5th, and 6th options in your code, you may use several elif conditions.

To run conditional sentences, we can use minimal code by declaring all conditions in a single expression.

If statement can be nested.

5.1.1 If Statement:

The if statement in Python is used to make decisions. It includes a body of code that only executes when the if statement's condition is correct. If the statement is wrong, the else argument, which includes code for else conditions, is executed. If you want to explain one claim while the other is false, you use the if-else expression in Python.

Syntax:

if expression

 Statement

else

 Statement

If-else flowchart:

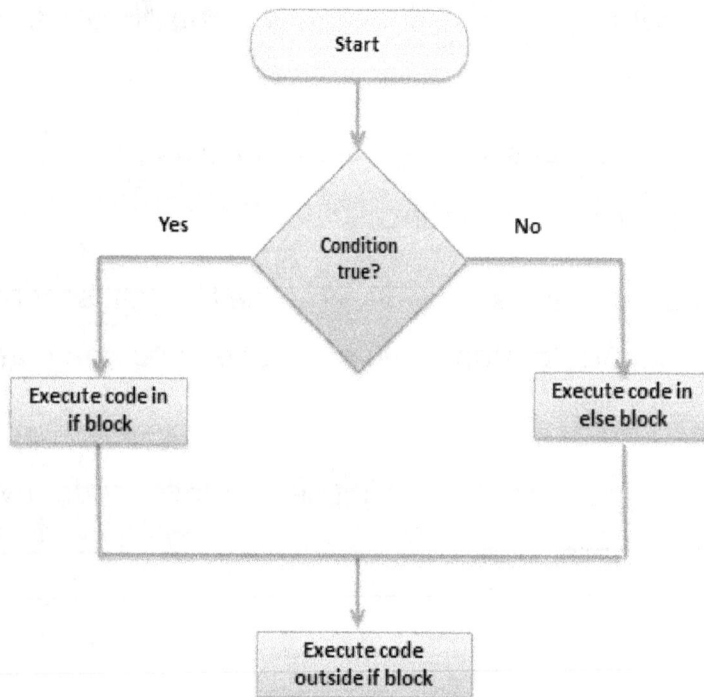

Example:

```
#
#Example file for working with conditional statement
#
def main():
    x,y =3,6

    if(x < y):
        st= "x is less than y"
    print(st)

if __name__ == "__main__":
    main()
```

```
x is less than y
```

5.1.2 Else condition:

When judging one sentence against another, the "else situation" is commonly employed. When one criterion fails, there must be a second condition that justifies the argument or rationale.

When "else condition" does not work:

There will be a number of times that the "else state" fails to provide the desired outcome. It would print the incorrect outcome due to a logical error in the software. In certain instances, this occurs where a program requires you to explain more than two statements or conditions.

The software outputs "x is greater than y," which is incorrect since both variables are the same (6,6). This is since the first condition which is if condition in Python is checked first, and if it fails, the second condition which is else condition is printed by default. We'll look at how to fix this error in the next step.

```
#
#Example file for working with conditional statement
#
def main():
    x,y =6,3

    if(x < y):
        st= "x is less than y"
    else:
        st= "x is greater than y"
    print (st)

if __name__ == "__main__":
    main()
```

```
x is greater than y
```

5.1.3 Elif condition:

We will use the "elif" expression to fix the previous error caused by the "else" condition. When you use the "elif" condition, you're asking the software to read out 3rd condition or probability if the first one fails.

```
#
#Example file for working with conditional statement
#
def main():
    x,y =6,6

    if(x < y):
        st= "x is less than y"

    elif (x == y):
        st= "x is same as y"

    else:
        st="x is greater than y"
    print(st)

if __name__ == "__main__":
    main()
```

```
x is same as y
```

5.1.4 Execute conditional statement with minimal code:

We'll see how to condense the conditional statement in this step. Instead of running code for each state individually, we may use a single code to handle all of them.

Syntax:

A If B else C

Example:

```
def main():
    x,y = 12,7
    st = "x is less than y" if (x < y) else "x is greater than or equal to y"
    print(st)

if __name__ == "__main__":
    main()
```

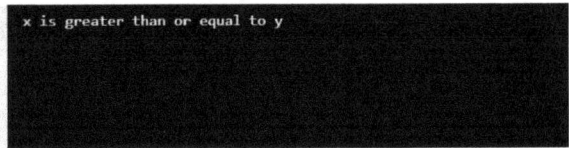

```
x is greater than or equal to y
```

5.1.5 Nested if Statement:

The following example shows how to use nested if statements in Python.

```
total = 100
#country = "US"
country = "AU"
if country == "US":
    if total <= 50:
        print("Shipping Cost is  $70")
elif total <= 100:
        print("Shipping Cost is $65")
elif total <= 150:
        print("Shipping Costs $5")
else:
        print("FREE")
if country == "AU":
    if total <= 50:
        print("Shipping Cost is  $100")
else:
        print("FREE")
```

```
Shipping Cost is $65
```

5.1.6 Switch Case Statement:

The value of a variable is compared to the values defined in the case of statements in a switch argument, which is an adjustable branch statement.

A switch declaration is not available in the Python programming language.

Switch Case in Python is implemented using dictionary mapping.

Example:

```
def SwitchExample(argument):
    switcher = {
        0: " This is Case Zero ",
        1: " This is Case One ",
        2: " This is Case Two ",
    }
    return switcher.get(argument, "nothing")

if __name__ == "__main__":
    argument = 1
    print (SwitchExample(argument))
```

```
This is Case One
```

5.2 Control flow statements:

The control flow of a computer is the sequence in which its code is executed.

Conditional statements, function calls, and loops govern the flow of control of a Python application.

There are three different kinds of control systems in Python:

Sequential - The default mode is sequential.

Selection - It is a decision-making and branching tool.

Repetition - Looping is accomplished by copying a bit of code several times.

Sequential statements:

Sequential statements are just a group of statements that are executed in a certain order. The difficulty with sequential statements is that even if the reasoning in each of the lines fails, the whole source code would fail to execute.

```
## This is a Sequential statement
a=15
b=9
c=a-b
print("Subtraction is : ",c)
```

```
Subtraction is :  6
```

Selection/Decision control statements:

In Python, selection statements are regarded as branching statements or decision control statements.

The selection statement helps a program to evaluate several criteria and perform orders depending on which one is correct.

Below are some Decision Control Statements are:

1. Simple if

2. if-else

3. nested if

4. if-elif-else

5.2.1 Simple if:

If statements being control flow statements that enable one to run a program only if a certain requirement is met or fulfilled. There is just one requirement to verify in a clear if.

Flowchart:

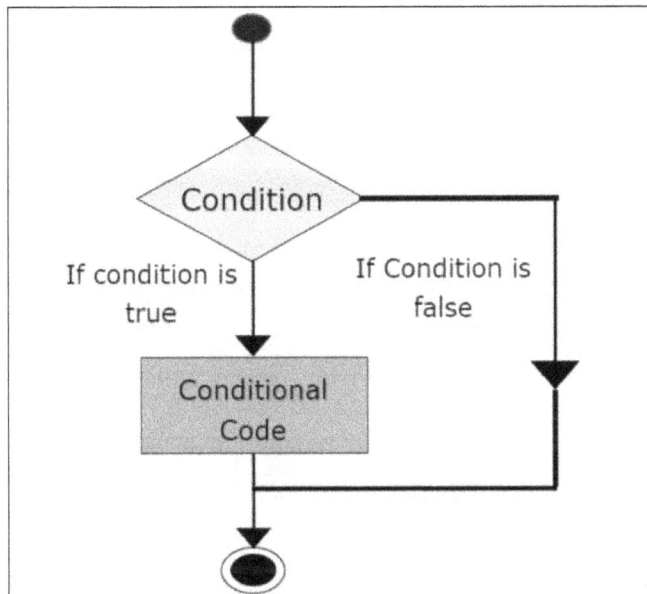

Example:

```
n = 10
if n % 2 == 0:
    print("n is an even number")
```

```
n is an even number
```

5.2.2 if-else:

If a test condition is True, the if-else argument tests the condition and executes the body of if, however, if a condition is False, a body of else would be executed.

Flowchart:

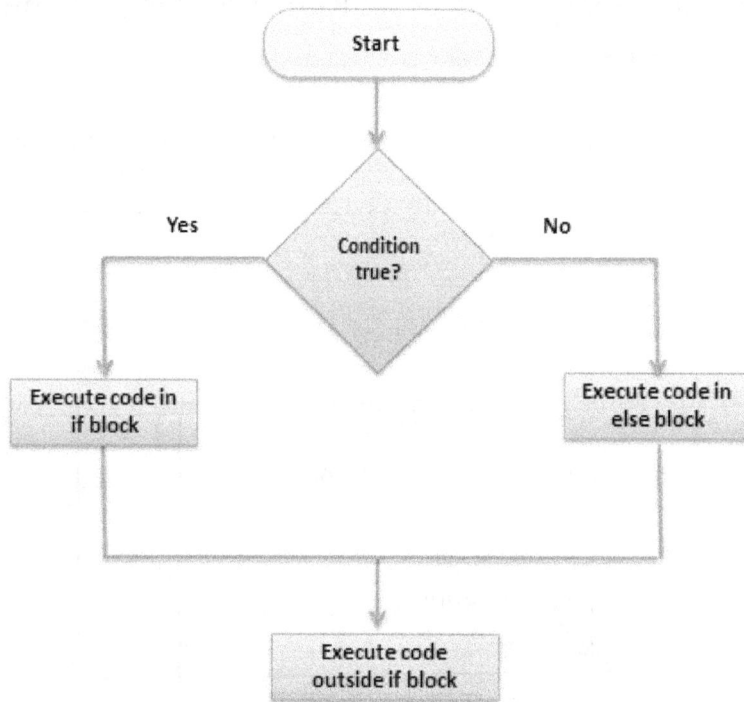

Example:

```
n = 6
if n % 2 == 0:
    print("n is even")
else:
    print("n is odd")
```

```
n is even
```

5.2.3 nested if:

An if statement within another if statement is known as a nested if statement.

Flowchart:

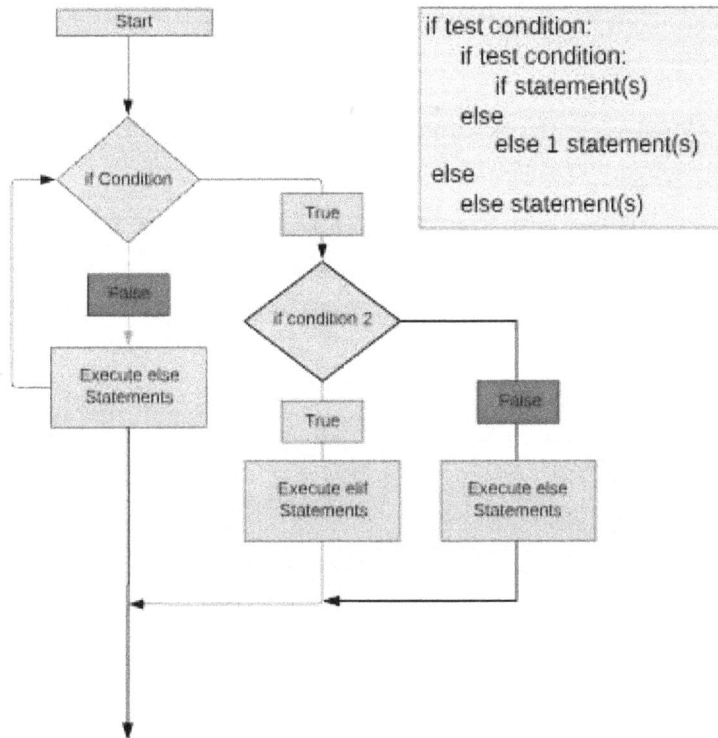

```
if test condition:
    if test condition:
        if statement(s)
    else
        else 1 statement(s)
else
    else statement(s)
```

Example:

```python
a = 2
b = 9
c = 18
if a > b:
    if a > c:
        print("a value is big")
    else:
        print("c value is big")
elif b > c:
    print("b value is big")
else:
    print("c is big")
```

```
c is big
```

5.2.4 if-elif-else:

The if-elif-else statement is required to perform a statement or block of statements in a conditional manner.

Flowchart:

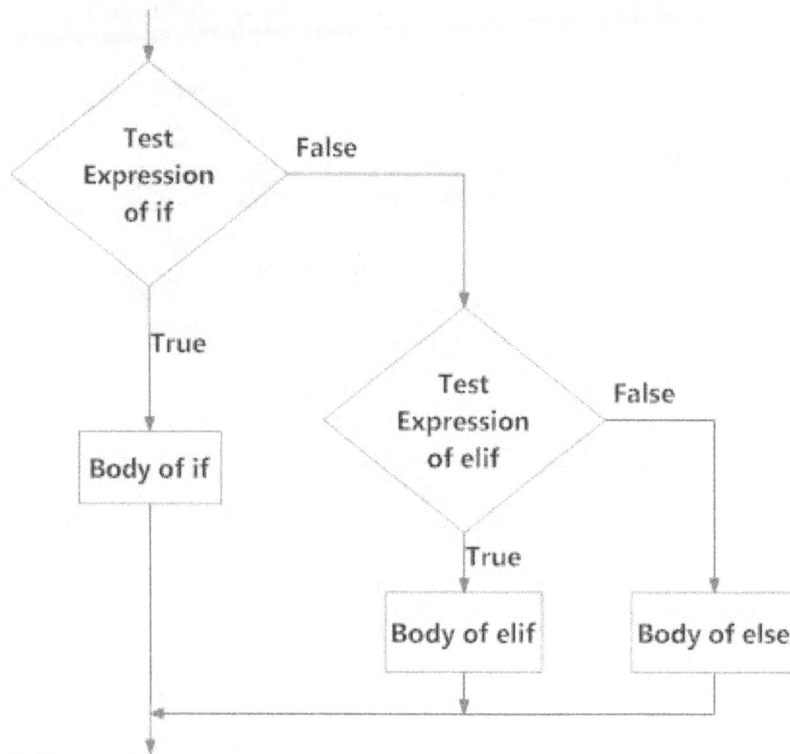

Example:

```
x = 25
y = 15
if x == y:
    print("Both are Equal")
elif x > y:
    print("x is greater than y")
else:
    print("x is smaller than y")
```

```
x is greater than y
```

Repetition statements:

A repeating argument is used to replicate a set of programming instructions (or a block of instructions).

We typically have two repetitive statements/loops in Python:

1. for loop

2. while loop

5.2.5 for loop:

Iterate over a series which is a list, dictionary, tuple, or set with a for loop. For each object in a collection, tuple, or dictionary, we may run a series of statements once.

Flowchart:

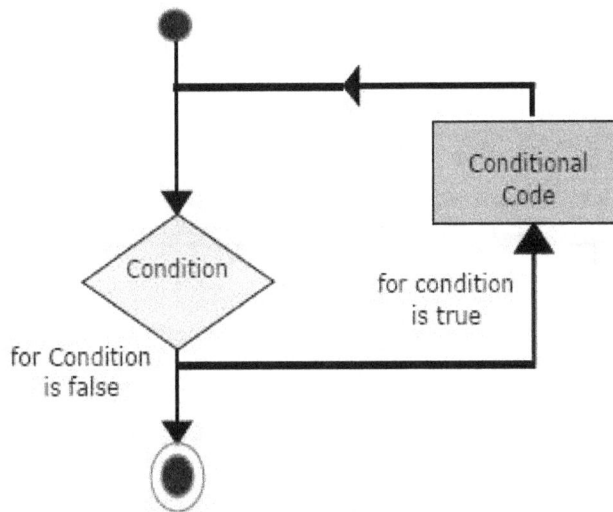

Example:

```
lst = [6, 7, 8, 9, 0]
for i in range(len(lst)):
    print(lst[i], end = " ")

for j in range(0,10):
    print(j, end = " ")
```

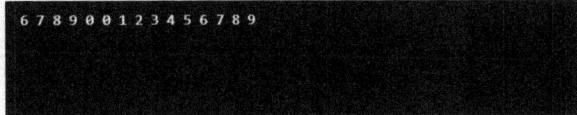

```
6 7 8 9 0 0 1 2 3 4 5 6 7 8 9
```

5.2.6 while loop:

While loops are used in Python to run a sequence of statements continuously before a requirement is met. The expression is then double-checked, and if it is indeed valid, the body is exercised once more. This process is repeated until the phrase is no longer true.

Flowchart:

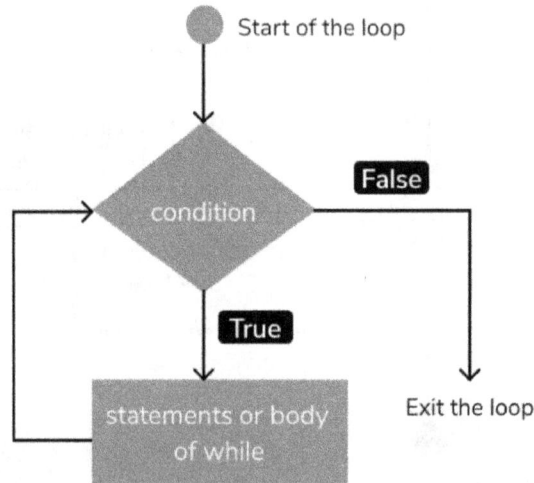

Example:

```
m = 8
i = 0
while i < m:
    print(i, end = " ")
    i = i + 1
print("End")
```

```
0 1 2 3 4 5 6 7 End
```

Chapter 6: Modules and Functions in Python

6.1   Modules:

The module is only an a.py Python file which may be loaded into another Python application.

The module name is the name of a Python file.

The module includes

- class descriptions and implementations

- variables

- features that may be found within other programs

Benefits of modules:

Reusability: Working with modules allows you to reuse your code.

Simplicity: Rather than dwelling on the whole issue, the module focuses on a specific portion of it.

Scoping: A module defines a different namespace that helps to prevent identifier collisions.

To create a function — The def keyword is used to describe a function.

Module Creation:

In this program, a function named "Module" is generated, and the file is saved with the name Python.py, i.e. the file's name, and the extension.py.

```
# Python program to create a module
# Defining a function
def Module():
    print("Hey, I am a Module")

# Defining a variable
location = "Python"
```

We've generated four functions in this program: addition, multiplication, subtraction, and division.

Importing a module:

```
# importing  module Operations.py
import Operations

print(Operations.add(10, 2))
print(Operations.subtract(15, 8))
print(Operations.mul(45, 10))
print(Operations.div(90, 5))
```

When the interpreter finds an import expression, it imports a module if a module is found in a search path.

6.2   Functions:

The function is a code block that only executes when it is named. Parameters are data that can be passed through a function.

As a result, a function will return data.

6.2.1 User-defined functions:

User-defined functions are functions that we assign ourselves to perform a given purpose.

As you can see in the Python.py file example above, we built our specific function to execute a specific task.

Advantages of user-defined functions:

User-defined functions enable you to break down a complex application into smaller chunks, making it easier to learn, manage, and debug.

If a program contains repetitive code; a function may be required to include certain codes and call them when they are required.

6.2.2 Built-in Functions :

Python has many functions that can be used right away. These are referred to as built-in features.

```
abs(),delattr(),hash(),memoryview(),set(),all(),dict(),help(),min(),seta
ttr(),any(),dir(),hex(),next(),slice(),ascii(),divmod(),id(),object(),so
rted(),bin(),enumerate(),input(),oct(),staticmethod(),bool(),eval(),int(
),open(),str(),breakpoint(),exec(),isinstance(),ord(),sum(),bytearray(),
filter(),issubclass(),pow(),super(),bytes(),float(),iter(),print()tuple(
),callable(),format(),len(),property(),type(),chr(),frozenset(),list(),r
ange(),vars(),classmethod(),getattr(),locals(),repr(),zip(),compile(),gl
obals(),map(),reversed(),__import__(),complex(),hasattr(),max(),round()
```

- abs() returns a number's absolute value. The absolute value of a negative value is positive.

- While all values in Python iterable have a Boolean value of True, all() returns True, otherwise False.

- a printable version of the python object is returned by ascii() (Python or a string list).

- bin() is a function that transforms an integer into a binary string.

- bytearray() returns a python array of the specified size in bytes.

- Python code object is returned by compile().

6.2.3 Lambda Functions :

Anonymous functions are those that are described without a name.

In Python, the def keyword is used to describe regular functions, while the lambda keyword is used to define anonymous functions.

Use of Lambda Function in python:

For a limited time, a nameless role is needed. We usually use this as an argument to a higher-order function in Python i.e. a function that takes in other functions as arguments.

Built-in functions such as filter(), map(), and others are combined with lambda functions.

filter() — As the name implies, this function is being used to filter iterables according to conditions. A filter takes the initial iterable and filters it, passing only the objects that return True for the filter element.

map() — Map applies all of a function's requirements to the objects in an iterable, allowing you to add a function to it, and then passing it to the result, which will have the same or different values.

```python
# Program to filter out only the even items from a list
my_list = [1, 5, 4, 6, 8, 11, 3, 12]

new_list = list(filter(lambda x: (x%2 == 0) , my_list))

print(new_list)

[4, 6, 8, 12]
```

```python
# Program to double each item in a list using map()
my_list = [1, 5, 4, 6, 8, 11, 3, 12]

new_list = list(map(lambda x:(x % 2==0) , my_list))

print(new_list)

[False, False, True, True, True, False, False, True]
```

As you will see in the software, we divided each factor by two and set its modulus to zero. The current array that uses the filter() only returns the numbers that satisfy the requirement, while map() extracts all entities in a Boolean form then returns True if the condition is fulfilled.

6.2.4 Recursion Functions:

A recursive function is described by self-referential expressions in terms of itself. This implies that the feature can keep calling itself and repeating its actions before a requirement is reached which causes it to return a response.

```python
def factorial(x):
    if x == 1:
        return 1
    else:
        return (x * factorial(x-1))


num = 3
print("The factorial of", num, "is", factorial(num))
```

```
The factorial of 3 is 6
```

It's a representation of a recursive function that finds the integer's factorial.

The product of all of the integers from 1 to that number is the factorial of that number. For instance, the factorial of 3 (written as 3!) is 1*2*3 = 6.

The function 'factorial' is called recursively until the condition is False.

Chapter 7: Files In Python

7.1   Files:

Files are called places on discs where similar data is stored. They're used to store the data in non-volatile memory for a long time (e.g. hard disk).

We use files for the potential use of the data by indefinitely saving it because Random Access Memory (RAM) is transient (it sacrifices its data when the device is switched off).

We must first open a file before we can write to or read from it. When we're finished, it needs to close so that the file's resources can be published.

As a result, a file procedure in Python is carried out in the following order:

- Create a new file

- You may either read or compose (perform the function)

- Close the file

7.1.1 Opening Files in Python:

To open the file in Python, use the open() macro. This function returns file object, also known as a handle, which can be used to read or change the file.

>>> f = open("test.txt")   # open file in current directory

>>> f = open("C:/Python38/README.txt")

specifying full path

When we open a file, we may define the mode. We decide and if we want to read r, write w, or add a to the file in the mode parameter. We may also decide if the file should be opened in a text or binary format.

Trying to read in text mode is the default setting. When reading from the file in this phase, we get strings.

Binary mode, on the other hand, recovers byte which is the mode to use for working with non-text files such as photos or executable files.

```
f = open("test.txt")      # equivalent to 'r' or 'rt'

f = open("test.txt",'w')  # write in text mode

f = open("img.bmp",'r+b') # read and write in binary mode
```

The character a, unlike in other languages, does not mean the number 97 unless it is encoded via ASCII or other equivalent encodings.

Mode	Description
r	Opens a file for reading. (default)
w	Opens a file for writing. Creates a new file if it does not exist or truncates the file if it exists.
x	Opens a file for exclusive creation. If the file already exists, the operation fails.
a	Opens a file for appending at the end of the file without truncating it. Creates a new file if it does not exist.
t	Opens in text mode. (default)
b	Opens in binary mode.
+	Opens a file for updating (reading and writing)

Furthermore, the default encoding varies by device. In Windows, it's cp1252, but in Linux, it's utf-8.

As a result, we cannot depend just on default encoding since our code can act differently across platforms.

As a result, specifying the encoding type while dealing with files within text mode is strongly recommended.

```
f = open("test.txt", mode='r', encoding='utf-8')
```

7.1.2 Closing Files in Python:

We must correctly close the file after we have finished running operations on it.

When you close a file, the services associated with it are published. The close() method in Python is used to do this.

The garbage collector in Python cleans up unreferenced artifacts, but we shouldn't depend on this to close the file.

```
f = open("test.txt", encoding = 'utf-8')

# perform file operations

f.close()
```

This strategy isn't completely risk-free. The code escapes without shutting the file if an error happens when running any action with it.

Using a try...finally block is a better choice.

```
try:
    f = open("test.txt", encoding = 'utf-8')
    # perform file operations
finally:
```

```
f.close()
```

We should ensure that the file is correctly closed even though an exception is raised, causing software flow to halt.

The with declaration is the most effective way of closing a paper. When the block within the with declaration is exited, the file would be locked.

The close() function does not need to be called directly. Internally, it is carried out.

```
with open("test.txt", encoding = 'utf-8') as f:

    # perform file operations
```

7.1.3 Writing to Files in Python:

In Python, we must open the file in write w, add a, or exclusive development x mode in an attempt to write into it.

We must be cautious when using the w mode since it can delete a file that already exists. As a result, the existing data is deleted.

The write() procedure is used to write a string or a series of bytes, for binary files. The number of characters wrote to a file is returned by this process.

```
with open("test.txt",'w',encoding = 'utf-8') as f:

    f.write("my first file\n")

    f.write("This file\n\n")

f.write("contains three lines\n")
```

If test.txt does not already reside in the current directory, this software can build it. If it exists, it has been overwritten.

To separate the various sections, we must use the newline characters ourselves.

7.1.4 Reading Files in Python:

We must open a file in reading r mode in Python to read it.

This can be accomplished using a variety of techniques. To read in a size number of data, we can use a read(size) form. It reads then returns up until the end of a file if a size parameter is not defined.

The text.txt file was created in the previous section can be interpreted in the following manner:

```
>>> f = open("test.txt",'r',encoding = 'utf-8')

>>> f.read(4)

# read the first 4 data

'This'

>>> f.read(4)

# read the next 4 data

' is '

>>> f.read()

# read in the rest till end of file

'my first file\nThis file\ncontains three lines\n'

>>> f.read()

# further reading returns empty sting
```

"

The read() form, as we can see, yields a newline as 'n'. On more processing, we have an empty string until we hit the end of a file.

The seek() method may be used to adjust the current file cursor (position). The tell() process, on the other hand, returns our current location in number of bytes.

```
>>> f.tell()

# get the current file position

56

>>> f.seek(0)

# bring file cursor to initial position

0

>>> print(f.read())

# read the entire file

This is my first file

This file

contains three lines
```

A for loop may be used to read the file line by line. This is both effective and quick.

```
>>> for line in f:

...      print(line, end = ")
```

...

This is my first file

This file

contains three lines

All lines in a file itself contain the newline character n in this application. To stop printing two newlines, we just use the end parameter of a print() call.

We may also read individual lines from a file using the readline() tool. This procedure reads a file before it reaches the newline character, which includes the newline character.

```
>>> f.readline()
'This is my first file\n'
>>> f.readline()
'This file\n'
>>> f.readline()
'contains three lines\n'
>>> f.readline()
''
```

Finally, the readlines() function returns a tuple of the file's remaining lines. When the end of the file (EOF) is hit, all of these reading methods produce null values.

```
>>> f.readlines()
['This is my first file\n', 'This file\n', 'contains three lines\n']
```

7.2 Python File Methods:

For the file object, you can use a variety of methods. Any of them were included in the instances above.

Here's a compilation of all the methods in text mode, along with a short description:

Method	Description
close()	Closes an opened file. It has no effect if the file is already closed.
detach()	Separates the underlying binary buffer from the `TextIOBase` and returns it.
fileno()	Returns an integer number (file descriptor) of the file.
flush()	Flushes the write buffer of the file stream.
isatty()	Returns `True` if the file stream is interactive.
read(`n`)	Reads at most `n` characters from the file. Reads till end of file if it is negative or `None`.
readable()	Returns `True` if the file stream can be read from.
readline(`n`=-1)	Reads and returns one line from the file. Reads in at most `n` bytes if specified.
readlines(`n`=-1)	Reads and returns a list of lines from the file. Reads in at most `n` bytes/characters if specified.
seek(`offset`, `from`=`SEEK_SET`)	Changes the file position to `offset` bytes, in reference to `from` (start, current, end).
seekable()	Returns `True` if the file stream supports random access.
tell()	Returns the current file location.
truncate(`size`=`None`)	Resizes the file stream to `size` bytes. If `size` is not specified, resizes to current location.
writable()	Returns `True` if the file stream can be written to.
write(`s`)	Writes the string `s` to the file and returns the number of characters written.
writelines(`lines`)	Writes a list of `lines` to the file.

7.3   File Handling:

Python, like many other programming languages, facilitates file handling and helps users to read and write scripts, as well as perform a variety of other file-related tasks. The idea in file handling has been extended to a variety of other languages, however, the application is often complex or lengthy. But, like other Python principles, this concept is simple and straightforward. Python handles files differently depending on whether they are text or binary, which is crucial. Every line of code consists of a series of characters that together shape a text file. A special character named the End of Line or EOL characters, such as the comma, or a newline character is used to end - line of a file. It signals to the translator that the current line has ended and that a new one has begun. Let's begin with files for reading and writing.

Working of open() function:

To open the file in write or read mode, we use Python's open () feature. As previously mentioned, open ( ) returns a file structure. We use the open() method with two parameters, the mode, and the file name, if to read or write, to display a file object. As a result, the syntax is accessible (filename, mode). There are three different modes that Python offers for opening files:

The letter "r" stands for literacy

"w" stands for "write."

For appending, " a " is included

" r+ ", which can be used for both writing and reading.

a file named "python", will be opened with the reading mode.

file = open('python.txt', 'r')

This will print every line one by one in the file

for each in the file:

>   print (each)

It's important to remember that the mode claim isn't needed. Python may presume it is " r " by default if it is not passed.

Working of read() mode:

In Python, there are many ways to interpret a text. We will use a file to generate a string that includes all of the characters in the file. Check it out.

Python code to illustrate read() mode

file = open("file.text", "r")

print (file.read())

Another method of reading a file is to call the specific number of characters, such as reading the first characters of recorded data and returning it as a string.

Python code to illustrate read() mode character-wise

file = open("file.txt", "r")

print (file.read(5))

Creating a file using write() mode:

Let's look at how to make the file and how to use write mode:

In your Python environment, type the following to manipulate the file:

Python code to create a file

```python
file = open('python.txt','w')

file.write("This is the write command")

file.write("It allows us to write in a particular file")

file.close()
```

The close() command frees the device of this software by terminating all services in service.

Working of append() mode:

```python
# Python code to illustrate append() mode

file = open('python.txt','a')

file.write("This will add this line")

file.close()
```

Several many other commands throughout file handling can be used to perform a variety of activities.

rstrip(): This function strips each line of a file off spaces from the right-hand side.

lstrip(): This function strips each line of a file off spaces from the left-hand side.

When operating with programming, it is planned to have a clean syntax and exception handling. That's why, where necessary, including them in a sentence is a smart idea. This is useful since all open files would be closed immediately when one is finished using this process, resulting in auto-cleanup.

```python
# Python code to illustrate with()
```

```
with open("file.txt") as file:

        data = file.read()
```

do something with data

Using write along the with() function:

Along with the with() module, we may also use the write function:

Python code to illustrate with() alongwith write()

```
with open("file.txt", "w") as f:

        f.write("Hello World!!!")
```

split() using file handling:

In Python, we can even break lines using file handling. When space is found, this breaks the vector. You can break using whatever characters you choose. The code is as follows:

Python code to illustrate split() function

```
with open("file.text", "r") as file:

        data = file.readlines()

        for line in data:

                word = line.split()

                print (word)
```

There are also a number of other features that aid in the manipulation of files and their contents. In Python Docs, you can learn about a variety of other features.

Chapter 8: Intermediate And Advanced Projects In Python

8.1   Intermediate projects in python:

The year is 2021. We are all aware that the IT industry is rapidly expanding. Python's development in the sector has been about 40% from 2013 to 2020, with predictions that it will rise to 20% further in the next few years. In the last few years, the number of Python developers has grown by 30 percent. So there's never been a great opportunity to learn Python because there's no better way to learn Python than by completing assignments.

Remember that the majority of the projects are linked to GUI creation / Web scraping because knowledge of GUI is critical for any ML or DL project implementation, and web scraping is critical for gathering data for just an ML project.

1. Birthday Wisher

Our task is to write a Python script that will deliver the birthday direct message or email to all of our friends on one's birthdays.

Tech:

Pandas, Smtlib, Time, and Schedule

Procedure:

Make a CSV file with the following information: name, email, phone number, message, year, and time.

Get the year and date of your birthday using pandas.

Make a feature called send_email which can be utilized to submit an email. It accepts three inputs: text, post, and topic.

If a birthday year matches the present year, the email would not be received because it has already been submitted.

If today is a birthday, check to see if the present time is the same as the wish time, then submit the email with the send email feature and raise a year column by the one.

Using the Windows scheduler, the application will start at 12:01 a.m. every day, or using a cloud server (pythonanywhere.com) will have it run at 12:01 a.m. every day.

Code:

```
import pandas as pd
import datetime
import smtplib
from email.message import EmailMessage
import os

def sendEmail(to, sub, msg):
    print(f"email to {to} \nsend with subject: {sub}\n message: {msg}")
    email = EmailMessage()
    email['from'] = 'Abhay Parashar'
    email['to'] = f"{to}"
    email['subject'] = f'{sub}'

    email.set_content(f'{msg}')

    with smtplib.SMTP(host='smtp.gmail.com', port=587) as smtp:
        smtp.ehlo()
        smtp.starttls()
        smtp.login('Email','password')
        smtp.send_message(email)
        print("Email send")
    pass
if __name__ == "__main__":
    df = pd.read_excel("data.xlsx")
    print(df)
    today = datetime.datetime.now().strftime("%d-%m")
    #print(type(today))
    update = []
    yearnow =  datetime.datetime.now().strftime("%Y")
    #print(yearnow)
    for index, item in df.iterrows():
        #print(index,item['birthday'])
        bday = item['Birthday'].strftime("%d-%m")
        #print(type(bday))
        if(bday == today) and yearnow not in str(item["Year"]):
            sendEmail(item['Email'] ,"Happy BIrthday "+item["Name"], item['message'])
            update.append(index)
    for i in update:
        yr = df.loc[i, 'Year']
        #print(yr)
        df.loc[i,'Year'] = f"{yr}, {yearnow}"
        #print((df.loc[i, 'Year'])
    #print(df)
    df.to_excel("data.xlsx", index=False)
```

2. GUI calculator

Our goal is to create a calculator that could conduct arithmetic operations using Tkinter.

Tech:

Tkinter

Process:

Make a straightforward design for the calculator.

Each keypress is recorded and values are retrieved.

To test the processes, use the evaluation feature.

Clear the display by pressing C.

Define the DEL button's activities.

Code:

```python
from tkinter import *


def input1(event):
    text = event.widget.cget("text")
    # print(text)

    if text == "=":  ## When = is pressed evaluate all the operations
        try:
            # evaluating the result for str
            result = eval(str(value.get()))
            value.set(result)
        except Exception as e:
            value.set("Error")
            print("error", e)

    elif text == "DEL":
        try:
            fullstring = value.get()  ## get the number from the screen
            newstring = fullstring.replace(fullstring[-1], "")  ## Remove last digit
            value.set(newstring)  ## set the new number as value

            # print(newstring)
            entry1.update()  ## Enter the updated number    ## eg > 557 --> 55
        except Exception as e:
            print(e)

    elif text == "C":
        value.set("")  ## set the screen as blank
        entry1.update()  ## update the screen
    else:
        value.set(value.get() + text)
        entry1.update()


root = Tk()
root.geometry("430x380")
root.title("Karl Calculator")
root.wm_iconbitmap("profile.ico")
value = StringVar()
entryframe = Frame(root, borderwidth=3, relief=SUNKEN)
entry1 = Entry(entryframe, font="lucida 37 bold", textvariable=value)
entry1.pack()
entryframe.pack(pady=20, padx=5)

buttonframe = Frame(root,)

list1 = [
    "9",
    "8",
    "7",
    "C",
    "6",
    "5",
    "4",
    "/",
    "3",
    "2",
    "1",
    "*",
    "00",
    "0",
    ".",
    "-",
    "%",
    "DEL",
    "=",
    "+",
]
i = 0
for n in list1:
    button1 = Button(buttonframe, text=n, font="lucida 28 ", padx=35, width=1,)
    button1.grid(row=int(i / 4), column=i % 4)
    i = i + 1

    button1.bind("<Button-1>", input1)

buttonframe.pack()

root.mainloop()
```

3. Language Translator

The project aims to develop a language converter utilizing the Google Trans library.

Tech:

Tkinter, google trans

Process:

Create a simple graphical user interface (GUI) for taking input languages and displaying output languages.

Pick a language using a dropdown or Combobox.

Create a feature that uses Google Trans to convert the input language or text into the output language.

Whenever a translate button is pressed, call the function.

Code:

```
from tkinter import *
from tkinter import ttk
from googletrans import Translator , LANGUAGES

root = Tk()
root.iconbitmap("profile.ico")
root.geometry('1080x350')
root.resizable(0,0)
root.title("Karl Language Translator")
root.config(bg = 'ghost white')

#heading
Label(root, text = "LANGUAGE TRANSLATOR", font = "arial 20 bold", bg='white smoke').pack()


# TEXT WIDGET
Label(root,text ="Enter Text", font = 'arial 13 bold', bg ='white smoke').place(x=200,y=60)
Input_text = Text(root,font = 'arial 10', height = 11, wrap = WORD, padx=5, pady=5, width = 60)
Input_text.place(x=30,y = 100)


Label(root,text ="Output", font = 'arial 13 bold', bg ='white smoke').place(x=780,y=60)
Output_text = Text(root,font = 'arial 10', height = 11, wrap = WORD, padx=5, pady= 5, width =60)
Output_text.place(x = 600 , y = 100)

### DropDown  #####
language = list(LANGUAGES.values())

input_lang = ttk.Combobox(root, values= language, width =25)
input_lang.place(x=20,y=60)
input_lang.set('choose input language')

trans_lang = ttk.Combobox(root, values= language, width =25)
trans_lang.place(x=890,y=60)
trans_lang.set('choose output language')

######## function that translate the text ########

def Translate():
    translator = Translator()
    translated=translator.translate(text= Input_text.get(1.0, END) , src = input_lang.get(), dest = trans_lang.get())
    Output_text.delete(1.0, END)
    Output_text.insert(END, translated.text)

######### Translate Button #########

trans_btn = Button(root, text = 'Translate',font = 'arial 12 bold', fg="white",pady = 5,command = Translate , bg = 'blue', activebackground = 'sky blue')
trans_btn.place(x = 490, y = 180)


root.mainloop()
```

4. YouTube Downloader

Our goal is to build a user interface that allows us to quickly import YouTube videos.

Tech:

Tkinter, pytube

Process:

Create the shortest user interface for receiving a video link as data.

Create various functions for beginning the update, displaying a progress bar, completing the download, and clicking a button.

The URL is passed to the start download() method by the button clicked function, which validates it.

start download() initiates the download and saves the file to the fixed destination.

The progress bar() function is used to display the download progress bar.

When the download is over, complete download() is called to view the download full code.

Code:

```python
from pytube import YouTube
from tkinter.filedialog import *
from tkinter.messagebox import *
from tkinter import *
from threading import *
font = ('verdana', 28)
file_size = 0


# oncomplete callback function
def completeDownload(stream=None, file_path=None):
    print("download completed")
    showinfo("Message", "File has been downloaded...")
    downloadBtn['text'] = "Download Video"
    downloadBtn['state'] = "active"
    urlField.delete(0, END)


# onprogress callbackfunction
def progressDownload(stream=None, chunk=None, bytes_remaining=None):
    percent = (100 * ((file_size - bytes_remaining) / file_size))
    downloadBtn['text'] = "[:.00.0f]% downloaded ".format(percent)


# download function
def startDownload(url):
    global file_size
    path_to_save = askdirectory()
    if path_to_save is None:
        return

    try:
        yt = YouTube(url)
        st = yt.streams.first()

        yt.register_on_complete_callback(completeDownload)
        yt.register_on_progress_callback(progressDownload)

        file_size = st.filesize
        st.download(output_path=path_to_save)

    except Exception as e:
        print(e)
        print("something went wrong")


def btnClicked():
    try:
        downloadBtn['text'] = "Please wait..."
        downloadBtn['state'] = 'disabled'
        url = urlField.get()
        if url == '':
            return
        print(url)
        thread = Thread(target=startDownload, args=(url,))
        thread.start()

    except Exception as e:
        print(e)


# gui coding
root = Tk()
root.title("Karl Youtube downloader")
root.iconbitmap("img/icon.ico")
root.geometry("500x250")

# main icon section
file = PhotoImage(file="img/youtube.png")
headingIcon = Label(root, image=file)
headingIcon.pack(side=TOP, pady=3)
# making url field
urlField = Entry(root, font=font, justify=CENTER)
urlField.pack(side=TOP, fill=X, padx=10)
urlField.focus()
# download btn
downloadBtn = Button(root, text="Download Video", font=font, relief='ridge', command=btnClicked)
downloadBtn.pack(side=TOP, pady=20)

root.mainloop()
```

5. Scraping Google Results

Our task is to write a script that will scrape Google results based on a query.

Tech:

Bs4, Requests

Process:

Using pip, install Requests for Bs4.

To scrape data from Google, build custom URLs.

Determine any of the groups in which the result is saved.

Obtain and display the outcome.

URL Preparation:

- Base URL for Google: https://www.google.com/search?aqs=chrome..69i57j46j69i59j35i39j0j46j0l2.4948j0j7&sourceid=chrome&ie=UTF-8

- When we look for "what is python," the base URL switches to https://www.google.com/search?q=what+is+python&oq=what+is+python&aqs=chrome..69i57j46j69i59j35i39j0j46j0l2.4948j0j7&sourceid=chrome&ie=UTF-8&sourceid=chrome&sourceid

Then we will build a custom URL that will take a question and return data using each of them.

python = 'what is python'

Query = query.

replace(" ","+")

`URL=f`

https://www.google.com/search?q=query&oq=query&aqs=chrome..69i57j46
j69i59j35i39j0j46j0l2.4948j0j7&sourceid=chrome&ie=UTF-8

How to locate all of the groups in which the result is saved:

Google stores the data in separate classes, but I pointed out that the key 5 classes would hold nearly 90% of the Google information.

.RqBzHd

.AZCkJd

.e24Kjd

.hgKElc

.kno-rdesc span

Code:

```
from bs4 import BeautifulSoup
import requests

headers = {'User-Agent': 'Mozilla/5.0 (Windows NT 10.0; Win64; x64) AppleWebKit/537.36 (KHTML, like Gecko) Chrome/58.0.3029.110 Safari/537.3'}
def google(query):
    query = query.replace(" ","+")
    try:
        url = f'https://www.google.com/search?q={query}&oq={query}&aqs=chrome..69i57j46j69i59j35i39j0j46j0l2.4948j0j7&sourceid=chrome&ie=UTF-8'
        res = requests.get(url,headers=headers)
        soup = BeautifulSoup(res.text,'html.parser')
    except:
        print("Make sure you have a internet connection")
    try:
        try:
            ans = soup.select('.RqBzHd')[0].getText().strip()

        except:
            try:
                title=soup.select('.AZCkJd')[0].getText().strip()
                try:
                    ans=soup.select('.e24Kjd')[0].getText().strip()
                except:
                    ans=""
                ans=f'{title}\n{ans}'

            except:
                try:
                    ans=soup.select('.hgKElc')[0].getText().strip()
                except:
                    ans=soup.select('.kno-rdesc span')[0].getText().strip()

    except:
        ans = "can't find on google"
    return ans

result = google(str(input("Query\n")))
print(result)
```

6. Message Sender GUI

The main aim is to construct a graphical user interface (GUI) that allows us to send SMS to various cell phone numbers.

Tech:

API, Tkinter

Process:

Create an account for any free bulk SMS provider (fast2sms, Twillo) and copy the Python code to sending messages from either API or developer section.

Create a graphical user interface (GUI) that allows us to enter a mobile number and a letter.

Create a message-sending feature and paste the entire code here, along with the mobile phone number & message as data.

To see the status of a post, use the display data feature.

Code:

```
import requests
import json
from tkinter import *
from tkinter.messagebox import showinfo, showerror

def send_sms(number, message):
    ## if you are using some other sms bulk service just paste the whole python code here and the place where number and message is inset replace it with number and message.
    url = 'https://www.fast2sms.com/dev/bulk'
    params = {
        'authorization': 'YOUR_AUTHENTICATION_KEY',
        'sender_id': 'FSTSMS',
        'message': message,
        'language': 'english',
        'route': 'p',
        'numbers': number
    }
    response = requests.get(url, params=params)
    dic = response.json()
    #print(dic)
    return dic.get('return')

def btn_click():
    num = textNumber.get()
    msg = textMsg.get("1.0", END)
    r = send_sms(num, msg)
    if r:
        showinfo("Send Success", "Successfully sent")
    else:
        showerror("Error", "Something went wrong...")

# Creating GUI
root = Tk()
root.title("Message Sender ")
photo = PhotoImage(file = "C:\\Users\\abhay\\Desktop\\ChatBot\\engine\\profile.png") ## Your icon path
root.iconphoto(False, photo)
root.geometry("400x350")
font = ("Helvetica", 22, "bold")
textNumber = Entry(root, font=font)
textNumber.pack(fill=X, pady=20)
textNumber.insert(0,"Moblie Number")
textNumber.configure(state=DISABLED)

textMsg = Text(root,height=10,font=("Helvatica",14))
textMsg.pack(fill=X)
textMsg.insert(END,"Enter Message")
def on_click(event):
    textNumber.configure(state=NORMAL)
    textNumber.delete(0,END)
    textNumber.unbind('<Button-1>',on_click_id)

on_click_id = textNumber.bind('<Button-1>',on_click)

sendBtn = Button(root, text="SEND SMS",pady=5,padx=3, command=btn_click)
sendBtn.pack()
root.mainloop()
```

8.2   Advanced projects in python:

Advanced Python Projects is indeed a wonderful field for escalating and growing your goal of being the greatest victor in the future. Python programming language that, for the most part, is very easy to use in order to complete tasks more effectively and easily. Python is used by the rest of the IT companies as a result of this.

1. Corona HelpBot

A chatbot that will respond to the majority of your queries related to COVID-19 and FAQs. The WHO website https://www.who.int/ data will be used by the chatbot to have responses. This may assist anyone who needs additional knowledge or assistance in learning more about the virus. It employs the neural network along with two secret layers sufficent for these questions and answers that predict the pattern corresponds to the user's query and routes traffic to the node. Many trends from user questions may be applied to prepare it for better performance and to provide more information regarding coronavirus to a JSON file. The more you practice this bot, the more accurate it becomes. Since stemmed terms from the pattern are paired with the user query, you don't have to pose the same query as mentioned in the JSON file while using deep learning.

Tech:

NumPy

Python 3

nltk

Tflearn

TensorFlow v.1.15 (no GPU required)

Process:

The JSON is used with potential query trends and the preferred responses are to feed data to the chatbot.

WHO is the JSON file that was used for the project. My JSON file is called WHO for this project. The group under which all of those responses fall is specified in the JSON file tag. All potential query patterns are listed using patterns. The responses section includes all of the replies to the patterned queries. Machine learning algorithms and neural networks, as we all know, need numerical data. But our string list isn't going to cut it. We need a way to describe numbers in our sentences, this is where the bag of words falls in. We'll describe every sentence with a list that's the same length as the number of terms within our model vocabulary. Each word in our vocabulary will be represented by a place in the chart. If the place within the list is a 1, the word appears in our sentence; if it is a 0, the word does not appear in our sentence.

Code:

```python
import nltk
import numpy
import tflearn
import tensorflow
import pickle
import random
import json
nltk.download('punkt')

from nltk.stem.lancaster import LancasterStemmer
stemmer = LancasterStemmer()

 #loading the json data
with open("WHO.json") as file:
    data = json.load(file)

#print(data["intents"])
try:
    with open("data.pickle", "rb") as f:
        words, l, training, output = pickle.load(f)
except:

    #  Extracting Data
    words = []
    l = []
    docs_x = []
    docs_y = []
```

```python
# converting each pattern into list of words using nltk.word_tokenize
for i in data["intents"]:
    for p in i["patterns"]:
        wrds = nltk.word_tokenize(p)
        words.extend(wrds)
        docs_x.append(wrds)
        docs_y.append(i["tag"])

        if i["tag"] not in l:
            l.append(i["tag"])
# Word Stemming
words = [stemmer.stem(w.lower()) for w in words if w != "?"]
words = sorted(list(set(words)))
l = sorted(l)

# This code will simply create a unique list of stemmed
# words to use in the next step of our data preprocessing
training = []
output = []
out_empty = [0 for _ in range(len(l))]
for x, doc in enumerate(docs_x):
    bag = []

    wrds = [stemmer.stem(w) for w in doc]

    for w in words:
        if w in wrds:
            bag.append(1)
        else:
```

```
            bag.append(0)
        output_row = out_empty[:]
        output_row[l.index(docs_y[x])] = 1

        training.append(bag)
        output.append(output_row)

    # Finally we will convert our training data and output to numpy arrays
    training = numpy.array(training)
    output = numpy.array(output)
    with open("data.pickle", "wb") as f:
        pickle.dump((words, l, training, output), f)


# Developing a Model
tensorflow.reset_default_graph()

net = tflearn.input_data(shape=[None, len(training[0])])
net = tflearn.fully_connected(net, 8)
net = tflearn.fully_connected(net, 8)
net = tflearn.fully_connected(net, len(output[0]), activation="softmax")
net = tflearn.regression(net)


# remove comment to not train model after you satisfied with the accuracy
model = tflearn.DNN(net)
"""try:
    model.load("model.tflearn")
except:"""
```

```python
# Training & Saving the Model
model.fit(training, output, n_epoch=1000, batch_size=8, show_metric=True)
model.save("model.tflearn")

# making predictions
def bag_of_words(s, words):
    bag = [0 for _ in range(len(words))]

    s_words = nltk.word_tokenize(s)
    s_words = [stemmer.stem(word.lower()) for word in s_words]

    for se in s_words:
        for i, w in enumerate(words):
            if w == se:
                bag[i] = 1

    return numpy.array(bag)


def chat():
    print("""Start talking with the bot and ask your
    queries about Corona-virus(type quit to stop)!""")

    while True:
        inp = input("You: ")
        if inp.lower() == "quit":
            break

        results = model.predict([bag_of_words(inp, words)])[0]
        results_index = numpy.argmax(results)
```

```
#print(results_index)
tag = l[results_index]
if results[results_index] > 0.7:
    for tg in data["intents"]:
        if tg['tag'] == tag:
            responses = tg['responses']

    print(random.choice(responses))
else:
    print("I am sorry but I can't understand")

chat()
```

2. Tweet using Python

Users will share and connect with tweets on Twitter, social networking sites, and online news. These messages are referred to as "tweets." Twitter is regarded as the "robot social networking forum." We will use Python to publish tweets without having to go to a page. The Python API is accessed through the tweepy library, which is a Python script. We'll do the same thing for tweepy in this case. Tweepy is a third-party library. Before you can use it, you must first update it. When you have pip, installation is a breeze. To install tweepy, type the command in the Command Prompt or Terminal.

Process:

Install pip as an extra library if you don't already have it.

Don't hesitate to adjust the program form in the settings from "Read-only" to "Read and write." This even grants the ability to tweet.

Go to https://apps.twitter.com/ after that. This is how the script and Twitter communicate with each other. Get a Consumer Key: API Key, Consumer Secret: API Secret, Access Token, including Access Token Secret from the "

Access Tokens and Keys" page. This is a straightforward approach for sending the tweet "Hello Everybody!" This is a simple procedure of no use in actual life. For any valuable work, it is merged into larger systems. To tweet a huge number of messages, we may use the for a loop. We may use the sleep() function from the time module to preserve the time interval between any 2 different tweets in the loop, as shown.

time.sleep(600) # waits for 600 seconds

It all came down to sending a text tweet. If we want to send a tweet that includes a media file, we'll need to use a different method.

A consumer can choose to upload a tweet that includes a media file, which is easy to do using the website GUI. Using Python to make a post requires some work. With only two lines of javascript, it's the same as sending a text-only tweet. Please remember to update the Application form to the one mentioned above. We won't be able to publish without it being changed.

Code:

Posting a simple tweet

```python
# importing the module
import tweepy

# personal details
consumer_key ="xxxxxxxxxxxxxxxx"
consumer_secret ="xxxxxxxxxxxxxxxx"
access_token ="xxxxxxxxxxxxxxxx"
access_token_secret ="xxxxxxxxxxxxxxxx"

# authentication of consumer key and secret
auth = tweepy.OAuthHandler(consumer_key, consumer_secret)

# authentication of access token and secret
auth.set_access_token(access_token, access_token_secret)
api = tweepy.API(auth)

# update the status
api.update_status(status ="Hello Everyone !")
```

Posting a tweet with a media file

```python
# importing the module
import tweepy

# personal information
consumer_key ="xxxxxxxxxxxxxxxx"
consumer_secret ="xxxxxxxxxxxxxxxx"
access_token ="xxxxxxxxxxxxxxxx"
access_token_secret ="xxxxxxxxxxxxxxxx"

# authentication
auth = tweepy.OAuthHandler(consumer_key, consumer_secret)
auth.set_access_token(access_token, access_token_secret)

api = tweepy.API(auth)
tweet ="Text part of the tweet" # toDo
image_path ="path of the image" # toDo

# to attach the media file
status = api.update_with_media(image_path, tweet)
api.update_status(status = tweet)
```

3. Send a message to Telegram user using Python

Have you ever heard how people use Telegram to automate tasks? You must be aware since Telegram has a large user base and is, therefore, one of the most common social networking platforms for reading people. What's nice about Telegram is that it has a lot of API methods, unlike Whatsapp, which has a lot of restrictions. So, in this article, we'll show you how to use Python to deliver messages to the Telegram customer.

Tech:

Telebot, telethon

Process:

To begin, use Telegram BotFather to build a bot. Take the measures below to make a BotFather:

Look for @BotFather in the Telegram software.

Send "/start" or press the start button.

Then submit the message "/newbot" to create a name and then a username.

BotFather will send you an API token, which is the bot token after you enter your name and username.

Then make a Telegram application. Follow the measures below –

Go to https://my.telegram.org to access the Telegram Centre.

Fill in the form under 'API implementation software.'

The API id and API hash parameters needed for user authorization will be returned.

For the script to function, you'll need to import many Python libraries.

telebot: In the terminal, type the following order to install this module.

pip install telebot

telethon (telethon): In the terminal, type the following order to install this module.

pip install telethon

Code:

```python
# importing all required libraries
import telebot
from telethon.sync import TelegramClient
from telethon.tl.types import InputPeerUser, InputPeerChannel
from telethon import TelegramClient, sync, events


# get your api_id, api_hash, token
# from telegram as described above
api_id = 'API_id'
api_hash = 'API_hash'
token = 'bot token'

# your phone number
phone = 'YOUR_PHONE_NUMBER_WTH_COUNTRY_CODE'

# creating a telegram session and assigning
# it to a variable client
client = TelegramClient('session', api_id, api_hash)

# connecting and building the session
client.connect()

# in case of script ran first time it will
# ask either to input token or otp sent to
# number or sent or your telegram id
if not client.is_user_authorized():
```

```
            client.send_code_request(phone)

            # signing in the client
            client.sign_in(phone, input('Enter the code: '))


        try:
            # receiver user_id and access_hash, use
            # my user_id and access_hash for reference
            receiver = InputPeerUser('user_id', 'user_hash')

            # sending message using telegram client
            client.send_message(receiver, message, parse_mode='html')
        except Exception as e:

            # there may be many error coming in while like peer
            # error, wwrong access_hash, flood_error, etc
            print(e);

        # disconnecting the telegram session
        client.disconnect()
```

4. Predicting Air Quality Index using Python

Let's look at how to use Python to forecast the air quality index. Chemical pollutant amount is used to measure the AQI. We can predict the AQI using machine learning.

The index of air quality (AQI) is a regular monitoring index for air quality. To put it another way, it's a test of how air quality impacts one's wellbeing for a brief time. The AQI is determined using an average concentration of a certain pollutant over a certain time. Most emissions have 24 hours, whereas ozone and carbon monoxide has an 8-hour time interval.

AQI Level	AQI Range
Good	0 - 50
Moderate	51 - 100
Unhealthy	101 - 150
Unhealthy for Strong People	151 - 200
Hazardous	201+

Dataset:

It has eight properties, seven of which are chemical emission amounts and one of which is the Air Quality Index. PM2.5-AVG, NO2-AVG, PM10-AVG, NH3-AVG, SO2-AG, and OZONE-AVG are also separate characteristics. The air quality index attribute is a contingent one. Since the air quality index is dependent on the seven attributes. There is no need for preprocessing since data is numeric and there are no missing values. The aim is to forecast the AQI, then either regression or classification would suffice. Since our class mark is constant, we could use a regression methodology.

Regression is a guided learning method for fitting data into a specific range. In Python, below are several examples of regression techniques:

Ada Boost Regressor

Random Forest Regressor

Linear Regression

Bagging Regressor

Code:

```python
# importing pandas module for data frame
import pandas as pd

# loading dataset and storing in train variable
train=pd.read_csv('AQI.csv')

# display top 5 data
train.head()
```

```
 importing Randomforest
om sklearn.ensemble import AdaBoostRegressor
om sklearn.ensemble import RandomForestRegressor

creating model
 = RandomForestRegressor()

seperating class label and other attributes
ain1 = train.drop(['air_quality_index'], axis=1)
rget = train['air_quality_index']

Fitting the model
.fit(train1, target)
'RandomForestRegressor(bootstrap=True, ccp_alpha=0.0, criterion='mse',
                    max_depth=None, max_features='auto', max_leaf_nodes=None
                    max_samples=None, min_impurity_decrease=0.0,
                    min_impurity_split=None, min_samples_leaf=1,
                    min_samples_split=2, min_weight_fraction_leaf=0.0,
                    n_estimators=100, n_jobs=None, oob_score=False,
                    random_state=None, verbose=0, warm_start=False)'''

calculating the score and the score is   97.96360799890066%
.score(train1, target) * 100

predicting the model with other values (testing the data)
so AQI is 123.71
.predict([[123, 45, 67, 34, 5, 0, 23]])

Adaboost model
```

```
# importing module

# defining model
m2 = AdaBoostRegressor()

# Fitting the model
m2.fit(train1, target)

'''AdaBoostRegressor(base_estimator=None, learning_rate=1.0, loss='linear',
                n_estimators=50, random_state=None)'''

# calculating the score and the score is   96.15377360010211%
m2.score(train1, target)*100

# predicting the model with other values (testing the data)
# so AQI is 94.42105263
m2.predict([[123, 45, 67, 34, 5, 0, 23]])
```

5. Amazon product availability checker using Python

Python is indeed a multi-purpose programming language that is commonly used for scripting. Its applications are not restricted to solving complicated calculations; they may also be used to simplify everyday tasks. Let's assume we want to monitor the availability of every Amazon product, catch the best price when it becomes available, and notify the customer by email when it becomes available. Writing the Python script for it would be a lot of fun.

Process:

Before running the script, make sure you have the necessary libraries installed (as specified in the code). Even, if a product is not currently accessible, no email should be provided to the recipient. The consumer can have an Asin Id for a product he wishes to monitor.

Each module's operation is as follows:

requests: Used to send and receive HTTP requests.

time: Used to determine the actual time, to wait, and to sleep.

schedule: This command is used to schedule the function to operate at certain times. It's similar to JavaScript's "setInterval" feature.

smptlib: A Python library for sending an email.

Code:

```python
# Python script for Amazon product availability checker
# importing libraries
from lxml import html
import requests
from time import sleep
import time
import schedule
import smtplib

# Email id for who want to check availability
receiver_email_id = "EMAIL_ID_OF_USER"


def check(url):
    headers = {'User-Agent': 'Mozilla/5.0 (X11; Linux x86_64) AppleWebKit/53

    # adding headers to show that you are
    # a browser who is sending GET request
    page = requests.get(url, headers = headers)
    for i in range(20):
        # because continuous checks in
        # milliseconds or few seconds
        # blocks your request
        sleep(3)

        # parsing the html content
        doc = html.fromstring(page.content)

        # checking availaility
        XPATH_AVAILABILITY = '//div[@id ="availability"]//text()'
```

```python
        RAw_AVAILABILITY = doc.xpath(XPATH_AVAILABILITY)
        AVAILABILITY = ''.join(RAw_AVAILABILITY).strip() if RAw_AVAILABILITY
        return AVAILABILITY


def sendemail(ans, product):
    GMAIL_USERNAME = "YOUR_GMAIL_ID"
    GMAIL_PASSWORD = "YOUR_GMAIL_PASSWORD"

    recipient = receiver_email_id
    body_of_email = ans
    email_subject = product + ' product availability'

    # creates SMTP session
    s = smtplib.SMTP('smtp.gmail.com', 587)

    # start TLS for security
    s.starttls()

    # Authentication
    s.login(GMAIL_USERNAME, GMAIL_PASSWORD)

    # message to be sent
    headers = "\r\n".join(["from: " + GMAIL_USERNAME,
                        "subject: " + email_subject,
                        "to: " + recipient,
                        "mime-version: 1.0",
                        "content-type: text/html"])


    content = headers + "\r\n\r\n" + body_of_email
```

```python
        s.sendmail(GMAIL_USERNAME, recipient, content)
        s.quit()


def ReadAsin():
    # Asin Id is the product Id which
    # needs to be provided by the user
    Asin = 'B077PWK5BT'
    url = "http://www.amazon.in/dp/" + Asin
    print ("Processing: "+url)
    ans = check(url)
    arr = [
        'Only 1 left in stock.',
        'Only 2 left in stock.',
        'In stock.']
    print(ans)
    if ans in arr:
        # sending email to user if
        # in case product available
        sendemail(ans, Asin)

# scheduling same code to run multiple
# times after every 1 minute
def job():
    print("Tracking....")
    ReadAsin()

schedule.every(1).minutes.do(job)


  while True:

      # running all pending tasks/jobs
      schedule.run_pending()
      time.sleep(1)
```

Chapter 9: Projects

Following are some main projects of python for beginners:

9.1 Rock Paper Scissors Game Project

The aim of a rock paper scissor program of python is to develop a one-player video game that can be played anywhere and at any time. This project is focused on the following guidelines:

Since rock unsharps scissors, rock emerges victorious.

Scissors benefit when they break the file.

As a result, paper triumphs.

Indicated project was created with the help of random modules, tkinter, and the fundamentals of Python.

Plays must select between rock, paper, & scissors in this python project. Then, by pressing the play icon, the game's outcome would be shown.

Requirements:

We will follow the primary concept with a random module and tkinter to execute a python rock paper scissors project of python.

Tkinter is a basic GUI library that makes it simple to create the graphical user interface.

To produce random numbers, use the random module.

We will use the pip installer command at the command prompt to load the libraries:

pip install tkinter

pip install random

Process:

These are the steps to make a python rock-paper-scissors game:

- Import the necessary libraries.

- Create a new window

- User-friendly code

- Code for choosing a computer

- Functions must be defined.

- Define a set of buttons

Functions:

Tk() is used to start Tkinter and generate a window.

geometry() makes the window resizable in width and height

resizable(0,0) command allows one to change the window's size.

title() is used to change the window's title.

bg = ''use to change the background color

When we want to show text that users can't alter, we use the **Label()** widget.

root is the name of our window

text that appears on a label as a title of the label

font to show the written form of text

pack is used to arrange widgets in block shape

user_take is a string variable that keeps track of the user's selection.

As we want to construct an input text sector, we use the **Entry()** widget.

The **random.randint()** method can choose any number from a specified set at random.

By halting the mainloop, **root.destroy()** would terminate the rock paper scissors program.

If we want to show a button, we use the **Button()** widget.

When the button is pressed, the **command** invokes a particular purpose.

When we run our code, the **root.mainloop()** function is called.

Code:

```python
#import library
from tkinter import *
import random

#initialize window
root = Tk()
root.geometry('400x400')
root.resizable(0,0)
root.title('DataFlair-Rock,Paper,Scissors')
root.config(bg ='seashell3')


#heading
Label(root, text = 'Rock, Paper ,Scissors' , font='arial 20 bold',
bg = 'seashell2').pack()


##user choice
user_take = StringVar()
Label(root, text = 'choose any one: rock, paper ,scissors' ,
font='arial 15 bold', bg = 'seashell2').place(x = 20,y=70)
Entry(root, font = 'arial 15', textvariable = user_take , bg =
'antiquewhite2').place(x=90 , y = 130)



#computer choice
comp_pick = random.randint(1,3)
if comp_pick == 1:
    comp_pick = 'rock'
elif comp_pick ==2:
    comp_pick = 'paper'
else:
    comp_pick = 'scissors'
```

```python
##function to play
Result = StringVar()

def play():
    user_pick = user_take.get()
    if user_pick == comp_pick:
        Result.set('tie,you both select same')
    elif user_pick == 'rock' and comp_pick == 'paper':
        Result.set('you loose,computer select paper')
    elif user_pick == 'rock' and comp_pick == 'scissors':
        Result.set('you win,computer select scissors')
    elif user_pick == 'paper' and comp_pick == 'scissors':
        Result.set('you loose,computer select scissors')
    elif user_pick == 'paper' and comp_pick == 'rock':
        Result.set('you win,computer select rock')
    elif user_pick == 'scissors' and comp_pick == 'rock':
        Result.set('you loose,computer select rock')
    elif user_pick == 'scissors' and comp_pick == 'paper':
        Result.set('you win ,computer select paper')
    else:
        Result.set('invalid: choose any one -- rock, paper,
scissors')




##fun to reset
def Reset():
    Result.set("")
    user_take.set("")
```

```
##fun to exit
def Exit():
    root.destroy()


###### button
Entry(root, font = 'arial 10 bold', textvariable = Result, bg
='antiquewhite2',width = 50,).place(x=25, y = 250)

Button(root, font = 'arial 13 bold', text = 'PLAY'  ,padx =5,bg
='seashell4' ,command = play).place(x=150,y=190)

Button(root, font = 'arial 13 bold', text = 'RESET'  ,padx =5,bg
='seashell4' ,command = Reset).place(x=70,y=310)

Button(root, font = 'arial 13 bold', text = 'EXIT'  ,padx =5,bg
='seashell4' ,command = Exit).place(x=230,y=310)

root.mainloop()
```

Summary:

Using Python, we successfully created the rock-paper-scissors game. For graphics rendering, we used the Tkinter library. To create random choices, we use a random module. We'll look at how to make a button widget. We even learn how to use the button to call the function. We developed a rock-paper-scissors python game in this way.

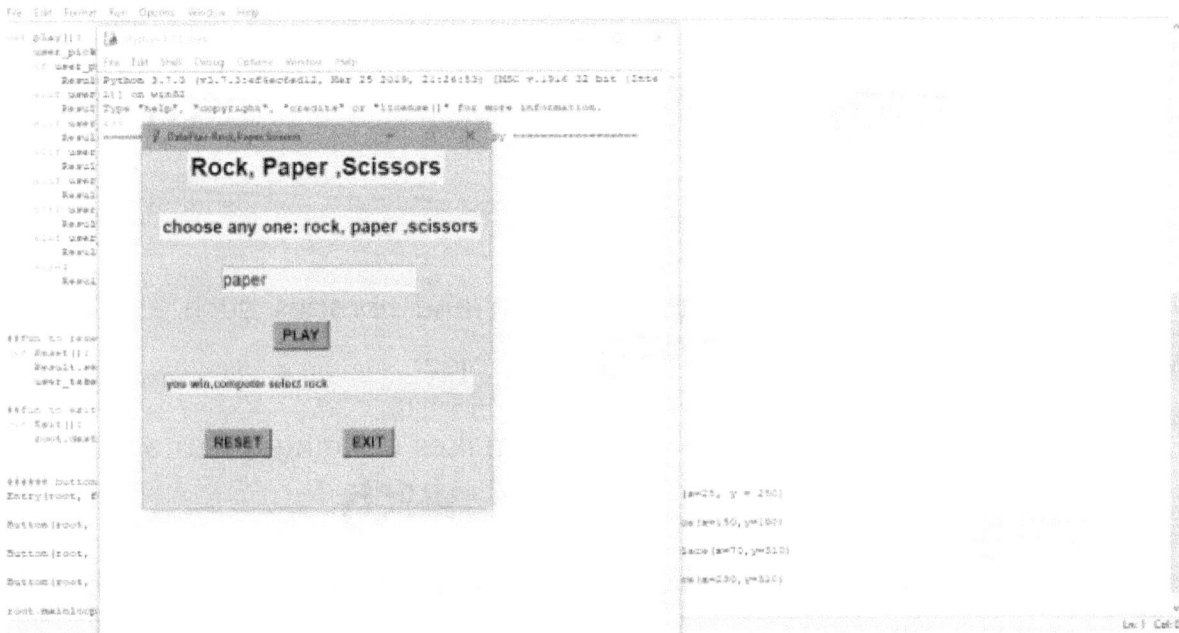

9.2 Python Password Generator

We all realize the passwords pose a serious security risk. Make your password difficult enough that no one will guess it to keep the account secure and protect it from being compromised.

It's a program that creates passwords regarding the rules you set in order to construct a solid, random password for the accounts.

The Password Generation tool generates a unique and random password for users, assisting them in creating a secure password with increased protection.

The goal of this project was to use Python to build a password generator. Python modules such as Tkinter, random, string, and pyperclip will be used to create the password generator project.

The consumer must first pick the password duration before clicking the "Generate Password" button in this project. The created password will be shown below. As the user presses the "Copy To Clipboard" icon, the password is immediately copied.

Requirements:

We will use some basic concepts of Python and libraries such as Tkinter, Pyperclip, Random, and String to build this project.

- Tkinter is a standard GUI library that makes creating a GUI application simple.

- The pyperclip module helps us to copy-paste text to or from your computer's clipboard.

- A random module can produce random numbers, while the string module has many functions for processing basic Python strings.

We will use pip installer from the command line to load the libraries:

1. pip install tkinter

2. pip install pyperclip

3. pip install random

4. pip install strings

Process:

Let's take a look at how to make a Python Password Generator.

- Modules can be imported

- A window has been set up.

- Define Functions

- Suggest password length

Functions:

Tk() generated tkinter, which implies that a window was created.

The height and width of the window are set by **geometry()**.

resizable(0,0) specifies the window's defined height.

title() changes the window's title.

The **Label()** widget is used to represent one or more lines of text which users cannot change.

The name which we relate to our window is **root**.

text is what appears on the label

the **font** is used to write the text

pack is a block of ordered widgets

The duration of a password is stored in the **pass_len** variable, which is of the integer form.

The **Spinbox()** widget is used to pick the password duration.

The **Spinbox()** widget is being used to pick a single value from a collection of options. The values range between 8 to 32 in this case.

The created password is stored in **pass_str**, a string style variable.

The empty string "" is used as a **password**.

The widget **Button()** was used to show a button on our browser.

When a button is pressed, the command is executed.

The **Entry()** widget is used to generate a text input field.

The latest text for the entry widget is retrieved using the **textvariable**.

The text was copied to the clipboard using **pyperclip.copy()**.

Code:

```
#importing Libraries

from tkinter import *
import random, string
import pyperclip



###initialize window

root =Tk()
root.geometry("400x400")
root.resizable(0,0)
root.title("DataFlair - PASSWORD GENERATOR")

#heading
heading = Label(root, text = 'PASSWORD GENERATOR' , font ='arial 15
bold').pack()
Label(root, text ='DataFlair', font ='arial 15 bold').pack(side =
BOTTOM)



###select password length
pass_label = Label(root, text = 'PASSWORD LENGTH', font = 'arial 10
bold').pack()
pass_len = IntVar()
length = Spinbox(root, from_ = 8, to_ = 32 , textvariable = pass_len
, width = 15).pack()



#####define function
```

```python
pass_str = StringVar()

def Generator():
    password = ''
    for x in range (0,4):
        password =
random.choice(string.ascii_uppercase)+random.choice(string.ascii_low
ercase)+random.choice(string.digits)+random.choice(string.punctuatio
n)
    for y in range(pass_len.get()- 4):
        password = password+random.choice(string.ascii_uppercase +
string.ascii_lowercase + string.digits + string.punctuation)
    pass_str.set(password)



###button

Button(root, text = "GENERATE PASSWORD" , command = Generator
).pack(pady= 5)

Entry(root , textvariable = pass_str).pack()

########function to copy

def Copy_password():
    pyperclip.copy(pass_str.get())

Button(root, text = 'COPY TO CLIPBOARD', command =
Copy_password).pack(pady=5)




# loop to run program
root.mainloop()
```

Summary:

We have successfully generated the random password generator project in Python using these measures. We learned about pyperclip and the random library when using the famous tkinter library to make graphics in the display window.

We learned to make keys, input textfields, markers, and spinboxes, among other things. We completed the password generator python project in this manner.

9.3 Hangman Game in Python

Instead of playing games produced by others, let's make our own in Python. Master the most common programming on the earth by working on the python hangman game. Heading back to our elementary school days, a few of the pen-and-paper games were still a favorite pastime of ours. Other than a few chit games, hangman needed players to guess terms based on predetermined guesses, and if they had missed all of their incorrect guesses, they were hanged, although on paper. Hangman is now played in a different manner. With recent technological advancements, we can now play hangman on our own machine without the need for another player.

Requirements:

This project necessitates a solid understanding of Python, including the ability to define functions and manage for/while loops. The functions we use here have arguments that are specified in the global scope and can be used in several functions to increase the quality of the game. It can further be used to offer different steps when the for/while loops are required to execute on certain conditions.

Process:

Let's start with the steps for creating a Hangman game in Python:

- The time and random modules are being imported.

- Functions with unique global arguments are described.

- To run the software, you'll need to use loops.

- Passing the feature to operate in the software.

So, in this Python project, we'll essentially do the same thing.

Functions:

Import random: It is used to choose an object at random from a list [] or a chain.

Import time: With this module, you can import the current time from your computer and use it in the software.

Time.sleep(): This function is used to pause the program's execution after a few seconds. It's a pleasant way to keep the game's player in anticipation for a brief period of time.

Global count, global show, global expression, global already guessed, global volume, and global play game are all initialized by the main feature. Based on how we wish to refer to them, they may even be seen in other functions.

Words_to_guess: This variable contains all of the Hangman words that the player is supposed to guess in a game.

Name: In this variable, we use a random module to select a word from the game's words to guess at random.

Length: The function **len()** is used to determine the length of a string.

Count: is set to zero and will increase as the code progresses.

Display: This displays the line for us based on the duration of the term we're guessing.

Already_guessed: The string indexes of correctly guessed terms will be stored here.

Play_loop: This feature takes the play game statement as an argument.

Play_game: This claim is used to either finish the battle after it has been completed once or to stop it based on the user's suggestion.

The play game argument is executed using a while loop. It accepts the values y=yes and n=no as parameters. If the consumer enters a value other than y/n, the query is reposed and the required response is sought. If the consumer enters "y," the game will restart; otherwise, it will stop.

Under the **hangman()** macro, we call all of the arguments once more.

Limit: This is the number of guesses we give the consumer for a given expression.

Guess: Gets the user's feedback for the guessed letter. Make an educated guess. strip() is a function that strips a letter from a name.

Code:

```
#                              Welcome to DataFlair Hangman Game:


import random
import time

# Initial Steps to invite in the game:
print("\nWelcome to Hangman game by DataFlair\n")
name = input("Enter your name: ")
print("Hello " + name + "! Best of Luck!")
time.sleep(2)
print("The game is about to start!\n Let's play Hangman!")
time.sleep(3)


# The parameters we require to execute the game:
def main():
    global count
    global display
    global word
    global already_guessed
    global length
    global play_game
    words_to_guess =
["january","border","image","film","promise","kids","lungs","doll","
rhyme","damage"
                  ,"plants"]
    word = random.choice(words_to_guess)
    length = len(word)
    count = 0
    display = '_' * length
    already_guessed = []
    play_game = ""
```

```python
# A loop to re-execute the game when the first round ends:

def play_loop():
    global play_game
    play_game = input("Do You want to play again? y = yes, n = no
 \n")
    while play_game not in ["y", "n","Y","N"]:
        play_game = input("Do You want to play again? y = yes, n =
no \n")
    if play_game == "y":
        main()
    elif play_game == "n":
        print("Thanks For Playing! We expect you back again!")
        exit()

# Initializing all the conditions required for the game:
def hangman():
    global count
    global display
    global word
    global already_guessed
    global play_game
    limit = 5
    guess = input("This is the Hangman Word: " + display + " Enter
your guess: \n")
    guess = guess.strip()
    if len(guess.strip()) == 0 or len(guess.strip()) >= 2 or guess
<= "9":
        print("Invalid Input, Try a letter\n")
        hangman()


    elif guess in word:
        already_guessed.extend([guess])
```

```python
            index = word.find(guess)
            word = word[:index] + "_" + word[index + 1:]
            display = display[:index] + guess + display[index + 1:]
            print(display + "\n")

        elif guess in already_guessed:
            print("Try another letter.\n")

        else:
            count += 1

            if count == 1:
                time.sleep(1)
                print("    _____   \n"
                      "    |       \n"
                      "    |       \n"
                      "    |       \n"
                      "    |       \n"
                      "    |       \n"
                      "    |       \n"
                      "__|__\n")
                print("Wrong guess. " + str(limit - count) + " guesses
remaining\n")

            elif count == 2:
                time.sleep(1)
                print("    _____   \n"
                      "    |     | \n"
                      "    |     |\n"
                      "    |       \n"
                      "    |       \n"
                      "    |       \n"
                      "    |       \n"
                      "__|__\n")
```

```python
            print("Wrong guess. " + str(limit - count) + " guesses
remaining\n")

        elif count == 3:
            time.sleep(1)
            print("    _____   \n"
                  "   |     | \n"
                  "   |     |\n"
                  "   |     | \n"
                  "   |       \n"
                  "   |       \n"
                  "   |       \n"
                  "__|__\n")
            print("Wrong guess. " + str(limit - count) + " guesses
remaining\n")

        elif count == 4:
            time.sleep(1)
            print("    _____   \n"
                  "   |     | \n"
                  "   |     |\n"
                  "   |     | \n"
                  "   |     O \n"
                  "   |       \n"
                  "   |       \n"
                  "__|__\n")
            print("Wrong guess. " + str(limit - count) + " last
guess remaining\n")

        elif count == 5:
            time.sleep(1)
            print("    _____   \n"
                  "   |     | \n"
                  "   |     |\n"
```

```
              "   |        |  \n"
              "   |        O  \n"
              "   |       /|\  \n"
              "   |       / \  \n"
              "__ | __ \n")
        print("Wrong guess. You are hanged!!!\n")
        print("The word was:",already_guessed,word)
        play_loop()

    if word == '_' * length:
        print("Congrats! You have guessed the word correctly!")
        play_loop()

    elif count != limit:
        hangman()


main()


hangman()
```

Explanation:

If the letter is accurately guessed, the index looks up the term for that letter. As per its index or what it belongs to in a given phrase, Display places the letter in a given room. If we have previously guessed the right letter and guess it once again, it instructs the person to attempt once more and does not reduce their odds. If the consumer guesses the incorrect letter, the hangman appears, along with the number of guesses remaining. Because the count was set to zero at the start, the value of each incorrect guess rises by one. The limit set to 5, and the number of assumptions left for the consumer for each incorrect feedback is (limit- count). The game stops as it hits the cap, displaying the correct guesses if any, and the term that was meant to be guessed. The consumer wins the game if the term is accurately guessed and matches the duration of the show argument. Play loop prompts the player to either continues playing the game or leave. If the play loop is set to yes, main() and hangman() will be restarted.

9.4 Dice Rolling Simulator Python Game

Python has a number of packages for creating a graphical user interface, or GUI. Tkinter is by far the most common, cheap, and simple Python package for creating graphical user interfaces. It is simple to use and has a versatile Object-Oriented Interface. Furthermore, when you create an app, you can use it on any device, reducing the number of changes needed to run it on Linux, Mac, or Windows.

We've always heard about dice. It's just a plain cube with numbers 1 to 6 printed on it. Although, exactly, what is simulation? It's the process of creating a computer model. As a result, the dice simulator is the basic machine model capable of rolling dice for us.

Requirements:

- Tkinter: Imported in order to use Tkinter to build graphical user interfaces.

- PIL (Python Imaging Library) was used to import Image and Imagetk. In our user interface, we use it to execute operations involving photos.

- Random: This is a feature that is used to produce random numbers.

Functions:

root – the name provided to the application's key window

text – text to be shown in a HeadingLabel

fg– the HeadingLabel font's color

bg– the HeadingLabel background color

.pack() – This method is used to cram the widget into the main window.

The term "dice" refers to a collection of picture names stored in the same folder that is selected at random using a random number generator.

The variable '**DiceImage**' is used to hold a picture of dice that is created by random numbers.

The '**ImageLabel**' function is used to display a picture in the browser. The parameter is set to True such that the picture stays in the middle even though the window is resized.

The '**rolling_dice**' feature is called if a button is pressed. When specifying a button, use the 'command=rolling dice' parameter to do this.

Code:

```python
import tkinter
from PIL import Image, ImageTk
import random

# toplevel widget which represents the main window of an application
root = tkinter.Tk()
root.geometry('400x400')
root.title('Data Flair Roll the Dice')

# Adding label into the frame
l0 = tkinter.Label(root, text="")
l0.pack()

# adding label with different font and formatting
l1 = tkinter.Label(root, text="Hello from Data Flair!", fg = "light
green",
        bg = "dark green",
        font = "Helvetica 16 bold italic")
l1.pack()

# images
dice = ['die1.png', 'die2.png', 'die3.png', 'die4.png', 'die5.png',
'die6.png']
# simulating the dice with random numbers between 0 to 6 and
generating image
image1 = ImageTk.PhotoImage(Image.open(random.choice(dice)))

# construct a label widget for image
label1 = tkinter.Label(root, image=image1)
label1.image = image1

# packing a widget in the parent widget
label1.pack( expand=True)
```

```
# function activated by button
def rolling_dice():
    image1 = ImageTk.PhotoImage(Image.open(random.choice(dice)))
    # update image
    label1.configure(image=image1)
    # keep a reference
    label1.image = image1


# adding button, and command will use rolling_dice function
button = tkinter.Button(root, text='Roll the Dice', fg='blue',
command=rolling_dice)

# pack a widget in the parent widget
button.pack( expand=True)

# call the mainloop of Tk
# keeps window open
root.mainloop()
```

9.5 Alarm Clock with GUI

The alarm clock is unquestionably useful for waking us up while we sleep, grab a short break, or alert us of jobs that we sometimes forget about. Our forefathers used alarm clocks dating back over 2,000 years, but technological advances have enabled us to hold the alarm clock without dial, gear trains, or other mechanical components.

The aim of this project is to use Python to create an alarm clock. Python has some really creative libraries, like datetime and tkinter, that help us create a project using current time and date as well as provide a user interface for setting the alarm in 24-hour format according to the requirement.

Requirements:

This project necessitates strong Python and GUI skills (Graphic User Interface). When Python is used in conjunction with Tkinter, creating graphical user interfaces is quick and easy. The Tk GUI toolkit has a versatile object-oriented framework called Tkinter. Since none of the modules included, unlike other libraries such as NumPy, must be downloaded beforehand, this project would be user-friendly and available in every virtual environment required for python programming.

Process:

Let's start with the steps for creating an Alarm Clock software in Python:

- Importing all of the required libraries and modules

- Introducing a while loop that takes the claim of the period the consumer needs to set an alarm for and immediately breaks until the time is finished, with music.

- Create a user input view pane.

Functions:

The **Tkinter** module is part of Python's basic GUI library. It enables us to build a dialogue box for whatever input we wish to provide or receive from users.

Python's time and **datetime** modules enable one to interact with and control the current day's dates and time while the user is using Python.

The **Winsound** module gives you access to the simple sound-playing capabilities of Windows platforms. This is good for making a sound as soon as a function is named.

Create an **alarm()** function that takes the argument (**set_alarm_timer**).

It has a while loop with the Boolean function True, making the program run automatically.

time.sleep(1) puts a hold on the rest of the commands until we get a time value from a consumer later in the code, and it returns the context thread of a clock ticking away at a constant interval.

Get the present time with **current_time**, which requires a datetime statement, **datetime.right now ()**. By string translation using **strftime(),** currently is used to print a present period while the date is used to display the **current_time().**

Create a new function called **actual_time()** that accepts a user value for the alarm to be set in string format. The same argument of **set_alarm_timer** as an alarm is used to start the while loop, which we can use later while creating the GUI.

If a user input time set alarm timer suits the while loop continuing time now, the notification would be printed as "Time to Wake up."

As soon as the condition is satisfied, **winsound.SND ASYNC** plays the machine-produced signal, which serves as an alarm clock alert.

Explanation:

Tkinter is initialized by passing a command with the word clock as a parameter (). DataFlair Alarm Clock is the name of the dialogue box, which has a geometry of 400*200. We use the time format to list a time format for 24 hours in the heading. The marking for a second heading is "Hour Min Sec" via addTime, which is provided just above user input boxes. To make the dialogue box appear more interesting, use setYourAlarm to add another mark that says "when to wake you up." Since we've already translated the current time to a string (actual time), we'll use StringVar to initialize the variables for a user input dialogue boxes (). Finally, create input boxes like hourTime, minTime, and secTime, which enable the consumer to enter the time the alarm should be set in 24-hour format. Submit executes a clock as a fixed button to begin the program, using the command of a given function actual time. Clock.mainloop() was provided as the first and last command to compile all of the previous commands with simple settings of color, font, distance, axis, and so on, and to view the window as early as the program is run.

Code:

```python
#                                           *Welcome to DataFlair Alarm
Clock*


#Importing all the necessary libraries to form the alarm clock:
from tkinter import *
import datetime
import time
import winsound



def alarm(set_alarm_timer):
    while True:
        time.sleep(1)
        current_time = datetime.datetime.now()
        now = current_time.strftime("%H:%M:%S")
        date = current_time.strftime("%d/%m/%Y")
        print("The Set Date is:",date)
        print(now)
        if now == set_alarm_timer:
            print("Time to Wake up")
            winsound.PlaySound("sound.wav",winsound.SND_ASYNC)
            break

def actual_time():
    set_alarm_timer = f"{hour.get()}:{min.get()}:{sec.get()}"
    alarm(set_alarm_timer)

clock = Tk()
clock.title("DataFlair Alarm Clock")
clock.iconbitmap(r"dataflair-logo.ico")
clock.geometry("400x200")
```

```python
time_format=Label(clock, text= "Enter time in 24 hour format!",
fg="red",bg="black",font="Arial").place(x=60,y=120)
addTime = Label(clock,text = "Hour  Min   Sec",font=60).place(x =
110)
setYourAlarm = Label(clock,text = "When to wake you
up",fg="blue",relief =
"solid",font=("Helevetica",7,"bold")).place(x=0,  y=29)

# The Variables we require to set the alarm(initialization):
hour = StringVar()
min = StringVar()
sec = StringVar()

#Time required to set the alarm clock:
hourTime= Entry(clock,textvariable = hour,bg = "pink",width =
15).place(x=110,y=30)
minTime= Entry(clock,textvariable = min,bg = "pink",width =
15).place(x=150,y=30)
secTime = Entry(clock,textvariable = sec,bg = "pink",width =
15).place(x=200,y=30)

#To take the time input by user:
submit = Button(clock,text = "Set Alarm",fg="red",width = 10,command
= actual_time).place(x =110,y=70)

clock.mainloop()
#Execution of the window.
```

Conclusion:

Congratulations on your achievement! You have finished the Python book for beginners in flying colors. You should be able to write intermediate-level programs in it at this stage. Both structure-oriented and function-oriented programming are supported in Python. It has dynamic memory management capabilities, allowing it to enable the effective use of computing resources. It also works for many of the major operating systems and architectures. As a result, both programmers would be able to understand this script.

Python is a popular programming language that can be used for a wide variety of domains and tasks. Python's high-level nature, user-friendliness and focus on accessibility, and improved code readability making it a great option among many developers worldwide.

Python can raise a syntax error or an exception if the information given is incorrect. The input function converts anything you type into a string. If an integer value is entered, the input() function converts it to a string. There are many options for output Formatting. In Python(3.x), a string modulo operator% is still usable, and it is commonly used. The old format style is no longer used in the language. Concatenation operations and string slicing are used to format this data. The string format approach necessitates further manual labor. If one of the criteria is valid or incorrect, the "if condition" is used to display out the answer. To run conditional sentences, we can use minimal code by declaring all conditions in a single expression. The value of a variable is compared to the values defined in case statements in a switch argument. Switch Case in Python is implemented using dictionary mapping. Python has many functions that are referred to as built-in features. In python, def keyword is used to describe regular functions, and the Lambda keyword is to define anonymous functions. Anonymous functions are those that are described without a name. Built-in functions such as filter() and map() are combined with Lambda functions. Files are places on a disc where similar data is stored. They're used to store the data in non-volatile memory for a long time. To open the file in Python, use the open() macro. We must correctly close the file after we have finished running operations on it. This strategy isn't completely risk-free. The code escapes without shutting the file if an error happens when running any action with it. In Python, we must open the file in write w, add a, or exclusive development x mode in an attempt to write into it. We must be cautious when using the w mode since it can delete a file that already exists. Python handles files differently depending on whether they are text or binary, which is crucial. Every line of code consists of a series of characters that together shape a text file.

This book has covered the essential fundamentals of the programming language to assist you in creating some useful Python snippets that will automate an easy yet tedious process and complete it in seconds rather than hours.

Python Programming

A Complete Python Guide To Introduction You In Programming With Exercise, Projects and Solution

By

Aiden Phillips

Introduction:

Python is a high-level programming language that is dynamically interpreted, symantic and object-oriented. Its high-level already present data structures, together with dynamic typing and dynamic binding, making it ideal for Software Development and as a glue language or scripting for the purpose of linking current components. Python's concise, easy-to-learn syntax prioritizes readability, which maintenance expenses for software. Packages and modules are supported by Python, which fosters code reuse and program modularity. An interpreter of python including its substantial standard libraries are available for free to download and disperse in binary or source type for all main sites.

Python has become a first-class citizen in contemporary infrastructure management, software development, and data analysis during the last several years. This is no more aside utility language, but instead a significant force in online application development and systems administration, as well as a primary driver of the machine intelligence and big data analytics explosions.

Python is popular among programmers because of the enhanced productivity it offers. The edit test debug cycle is extraordinarily rapid because there is no compiling phase. Python scripts are simple to debug: a bug or improper input will never result in a segmentation fault. However, when an interpreter finds a mistake, it throws an exception. The interpreter produces a stack trace if the application fails to catch the error. Inspection of global and local variables, execution of setting breakpoints, arbitrary expressions, stepping through a code one line at one time, and so on are all possible with a source-level debugger. The debugger is developed in Python, demonstrating Python's introspective capabilities. But on the other side, adding a few print declarations to a source code is frequently the fastest method to debug a program: the rapid edit test debug cycle helps make this basic method quite successful.

Chapter 1: Start to learn python

In comparison to other languages like Java, Perl, PHP, and Ruby, Python is a frequently used dynamic programming language. It's also known as the scripting language. It supports automated memory management, numerous programming paradigms, and incorporates object-oriented programming's fundamental notions i.e. OOP.

Python is a highly typed procedural language that comes with a large and comprehensive standard library. Python's library supports a variety of Internet protocols, including FTP and IMAP. It has a distinct grammar that distinguishes it from various programming languages such as C, Java, and C++. Python also has the following outstanding features:

- An open-source language

- A scalable and universal language

- The language is simple and straightforward to learn.

High-level language

It is a common misconception that the programming language's name is inspired by the snake Python. This is not the case. It comes from the title of a renowned television show called Monty Python's Flying Circus.

Python offers a lot of interesting uses. It's commonly utilized in complex content management software like the Django CMS and Plone, as well as frameworks like Django and Pyramid.

1.1 Why should you learn Python?

- Python is a simple language to learn. It has a simple syntax and code that is quite understandable.

- Python has a wide range of uses. It's used for web development, data science, and quick application development, among other things.

- Python is a computer language that enables you to develop programs with minimal lines of program code than many other languages.

- Python's popularity is steadily increasing. It's now one of the most widely used programming languages.

- Python is indeed a cross-platform computer programming language, which means it can operate on a variety of operating systems, including Windows, Mac OS X, Linux, and the Java and.NET virtual machines. It is open-source and free.

- While also Python comes pre-installed on most modern Linux and Mac systems, the version may be outdated. As a result, installing the most recent version is always a smart idea.

Run Python in the Easiest Way

1. The Thonny IDE is the most convenient method to execute Python.

2. The newest version of Python is included in the Thonny IDE. As a result, you will not need to install Python individually.

3. To install Python on your PC, follow the instructions below.

4. Thonny IDE may be downloaded here.

5. To install Thonny on your PC, run the installer.

6. Navigate to File > New. After that, save the file as an a.py file. For instance, hello.py, example.py, and so on.

7. You may name the file anything you like. The file name, however, must finish in. py

8. Fill up the file with Python code and save it.

9. Then choose Run > Run the current script and just press F5.

Install Python personally

Here's how to install and execute Python on the PC, if you do not like to utilize Thonny.

Install the most recent version of Python.

Run the installer and follow the on-screen instructions to install Python.

Check for errors throughout the installation procedure. Python should be included in the environment variables. Python will be added to the environment variables, so you'll be able to execute it from wherever on the machine.

You may also choose the location where Python is downloaded.

You may launch Python when you've completed the installation procedure.

Switch to Immediate mode in Python.

After installing Python, use python on the command line to start an interpreter in the immediate mode. To retrieve the result, we can simply write in Python code and hit Enter.

Enter 1 + 1 then press enter to see what happens. As a result, we obtain 2. You may use this prompt as a calculator. Enter quit() and hit enter to exit this mode.

Use an Integrated Development Environment to run Python (IDE).

To create a Python script file, we may use any text editing program.

All we have to do now is save it with the.py extension. Using an IDE, on the other hand, may make our lives much simpler. For application development, an IDE is a bit of software that gives beneficial capabilities like code suggestions, syntax checking and highlighting file explorers, and so on to the programmer.

Eventually, when people install Python, it comes with an IDE called IDLE. It will allow the user to access Python on any PC. For novices, it's a good IDE.

When you launch IDLE, it launches an interactive Python Shell.

You may now create the new file with the.py extension and save it. Hello.py is a good example.

Fill up the file with Python code and save it. To launch the file, choose Run > Run Module from the menu bar, or just press F5.

1.2 Python's Primary Benefits:

- **Python's success is based on several benefits it delivers to both novices and specialists.**

Python is a simple language to learn and use. The language itself has a small number of features, thus writing your initial applications will take very little time and effort. Python syntax is intended to be simple and easy to understand. Python is an excellent teaching language because of its simplicity, which allows newbies to pick it up fast. As a consequence, developers spend less time worrying about language complexity or understanding code left by others and more time pondering about the issue they're attempting to address.

- **Python is widely used and supported.**

Python is popular and extensively used, as shown by top rankings in surveys including the Tiobe Index and also the vast number of Python-based GitHub projects. Python is compatible with every main platform and operating system as well as the majority of minor ones. Python bindings or wrappers exist for many key libraries and API-powered services, allowing Python to easily interact with them or utilize them directly.

- **Python isn't a "toy" programming language.**

Despite the fact that scripting and automation account for a substantial portion of Python's use cases more on than later, Python is also used to create high-quality software, either as standalone apps or as web services. Python isn't the quickest programming language, but it generates for it in variety.

- **Python continues to progress.**

To stay up with contemporary software development processes, each release of a Python language introduces beneficial new functionality. Coroutines and Asynchronous operations, for example, are now standard elements of a language, making it simpler to develop concurrent Python programs.

What is the purpose of Python?

Python's most fundamental use is as an automation and scripting language. Python isn't only a substitute for batch files or shell scripts; it's also used in tools like Ansible and Salt to handle interactions with application GUIs or web browsers, as well as system provisioning and setup. However, Python's scripting and automation capabilities are only the tips of the iceberg.

Common application programming with Python

Python allows you to construct inter-platform and command-line GUI programs that can be deployed as standalone executables. Although Python does not have the ability to produce a solitary binary from the script, third-party tools such as cx Freeze and PyInstaller may help.

Machine learning and data science with Python

One of Python's most popular use cases is sophisticated data analysis, which has become one of the fastest-growing fields in IT. Python interfaces are found in the great majority of data science and machine learning libraries, making it the most widely used high-level command interface for different numerical methods and machine learning libraries.

RESTful APIs and Web services in Python

Python's third-party web frameworks and native libraries make it easy to build anything from basic REST APIs to full-fledged data-driven websites in a few lines of code. With the correct libraries, Python's newest versions offer significant contributions for asynchronous operations, allowing sites to handle hundreds or even thousands of requests every second

Code generation and metaprogramming in Python

Python treats everything in the language, particularly Python modules and libraries, as an object. This enables Python to operate as a very efficient code generator, allowing developers to create programs that control their functions and provide extensibility that must be difficult or even impossible in other languages.

Python may also be applied to drive code generation technologies like LLVM to produce code in all other languages more effectively.

"Glue language" in Python

Python is known as a "glue language," meaning it can connect unrelated pieces of code usually modules with C language interfaces. In this respect, it is used in machine learning and data science, although that's only one iteration of the overall concept. When you have apps or program domains that you'd want to link but can't communicate with each other directly, Python can help.

How does Python make programming easy?

Python's syntax is designed to be simple and easy to understand. In Python 3.x, a conventional "hello world" is really nothing more than:

```
print("Hello world!")
```

Various syntactical features are available in Python to represent many typical programs flows succinctly. Consider the following example program for lines reading from a text document into the list object while removing each line's closing newline character:

```
with open('myfile.txt') as my_file:
    file_lines = [x.rstrip('\n') for x in my_file]
```

A with or as construction is the context manager that allows you to quickly create one object for the block of code and afterward discard it outside of it. The object in this example is my file, which was created using the open() method. This replaces numerous lines of boilerplate for opening the file, reading specific lines from it, and then closing it.

Another Python quirk is a list comprehension, which is used in the [x... for x in my file] construction. It allows you to iterate over an item that includes other things as in this case, my file and the lines it includes, and every iterated element which is, each x is processed and automatically added to a list.

In Python, you could build a formal for loop just like you would in other languages. The idea is that Python offers a mechanism to describe things such as loops that iterate over several objects and execute a basic action on each element in the loop, as well as working with items that need explicit instantiation and disposal, in a cost-effective manner.

Python programmers may use structures like this to strike a compromise between brevity and readability.

The rest of Python's capabilities are intended to supplement typical use cases. Most recent object types, such as Unicode strings, are incorporated right into the language. Standard-issue data structures include lists, dictionaries (also known as key-value stores or hashmaps, tuples for storing immutable sets of things, and sets for maintaining collections of unique objects.

Python 2 vs. Python 3:

Python is offered in two versions, both of which are enough different to confuse many new users. Python 2.x, an older legacy branch, will be supported i.e., get official upgrades until 2020, after which it may be maintained informally. Many useful and significant features not present in Python 2.x, like additional syntactic features e.g., the walrus operator, stronger concurrency limits, and a more effective interpreter, are available in Python 3.x.

For the longest period, the absence of third-party library support hampered Python 3 uptake. Many Python libraries only supported Python 2, making switching difficult. However, the amount of libraries that solely support Python 2 has decreased in recent years; several of the most prominent libraries now support either Python 2 or Python 3. Python 3 is the best selection for new projects nowadays; you should only use Python 2 if people have no other option. If you're bound with Python 2 version, then please try a few different approaches.

There are no other programming languages that are as simple to use as Python. Other languages are clumsy and difficult to read. If you look at them closely, you'll see that they include a lot of brackets or even words that people won't recognize. It's enough to put someone off who isn't accustomed to programming since all of the terms seem to be scary. Python is a unique language. Besides all the wacky brackets, it uses indentations, resulting in a page that is simpler to read and less cluttered. It employs English instead of words you don't comprehend. The additional special characters have been reduced to a minimal level so that people may glance just at a page of code without feeling overwhelmed. It is one of the most straightforward programming tools available. It looks beautiful on the page and, where possible, will employ a lot of white space to make it simpler to understand what you need to know. If the software is too complicated for you, there are many locations with comments where you may receive an explanation. Overall, it's one of the perfect programming languages for getting ahead or learning the basics of programming. Because this software is written in English, it is quite simple to understand. There aren't many words you won't understand, and you won't have to waste hours trying to find out what its saying. The whole application is in English, and you'll be amazed at how easy it can make things. Python may already be installed on your machine in certain instances. Python will be installed automatically on Mac OS X and Ubuntu PCs. To get started, you'll merely have to download the text interpreter. All you have to do to use Python on a Windows computer is download the program. Python is compatible with all of these programs, even if it isn't installed right away.

People will just use Python on the own at first. It's an excellent program in which to learn and grow. However, you may decide at some point in the future that you want to pursue anything new that Python cannot do on its own. Fortunately, Python can interact with a variety of different programming languages, like JavaScript and C++, so anyone can play around, learn more, and obtain the code you need, even if Python can't do everything. You'll also need to get a text interpreter when you download Python. Python will be able to read your data more easily as a result of this.

You may use basic programs that are often already installed on a computer, like Notepad from Windows, or search for a more user-friendly interpreter. After you've decided on an interpreter to use, it's time to start creating code. Some people who are inexperienced in coding may be concerned about getting the code to function. Another place where Python can help is in this area. It might be capable of taking the words people are typing and, with the aid of the translator, throw them back out in a matter of seconds. While you're working on it, people can test what they are doing! There are several advantages to utilizing the Python software. Beginners will appreciate how accessible this program is and how quickly they can pick up on some of the basic commands. Even experienced programmers will be blown away by how well this all comes together!

Python is mostly used for:

- Web design and development

- System utilities i.e. command-line programs and system admin tools

- User Interfaces in Graphics like in Tkinter, Qt, gtk

- Embedded scripting

- Scripting on the internet

- Database programming and access

- Prototyping and development in a short amount of time

- Programming for games

Programming in a distributed environment

Chapter 2: Python variables

The variable is a designated place in memory where data is stored. Variables may be thought of as a container for data that may be altered later in the program. Variables are storage containers for data values. As an example, we've established a variable called number in this case. The variable has been given the value of ten.

```
number = 10
```

Variables may be compared to a bag in which books may be stored and changed at any moment.

```
number = 10
number = 1.1
```

The initial value of the number was ten. It was afterward updated to 1.1.

Creating a variable entails the following steps:

It is not feasible to declare a new variable in Python using a command. A variable is considered to be established when you first assign a value to it. Variables don't have to be allocated to a specific class, and they may change types after they've been established.

Variable Casting:

Casting can be used to specify a variable's data type.

Get the type:

The type() function returns a variable's data type.

Use single or double quotes?

String variables may be declared with single and double quotations.

A sensitive case:

The variables' names are case-sensitive.

2.1 Variables Names

A variable's name might be short, like x and y or it may be lengthy, like class, book name, or total inches.

Variables in Python have the following rules:

- A variable's name must begin with an underscore character or a letter.

- The initial character in any variable name cannot be a number.

- In variable names, both underscore like A-z, _, 0-9, and alphanumeric letters are used.

- Whenever it concerns variable titles, case matters: class, Class, and CLASS represent three different variables.

- Lowercase alphabets i.e. a to z or capital alphabets i.e. A to Z characters, numerals i.e. 0 to 9, and an underscore (_) should be used in variable names.

- Make a name for yourself that makes sense.

- If you wish to make a variable name with two words, separate them with an underscore.

- To declare a constant, use capital letters wherever feasible.

- Never use special characters such as !, @, #, $, percent, and so on.

- A digit should not be used to begin the name of a variable.

Variable Names with More Than One Word (Multi words):

Interpreting variable names with more than one word might be difficult.

You may make them easier to read in many ways:

Camel case:

Each phrase, except for the first, starts with a capital letter.

myVariableName = "Ali"

Pascal case:

Each word's initial letter is capitalized.

MyVariableName = "Ali"

Snake case:

Each word is separated by an underscore character.

my_variable_name = "Ali"

2.2 Organize/Unpack a Collection:

You may use this technique if you have an integer, tuple, or another group of values. Python facilitates the removal of values and the storage of those values in variables. Unpacking is the term for this process.

2.3 Output variables

In Python, the print expression is often used to produce values.

When text and a variable are combined, a + character is used.

The + sign may also be used to link any variable to the preceding variable.

For numbers, the + character acts as a logical operator. If you try to combine numbers and strings in Python, you may get an error.

2.4 Variables at a Global Level:

Variables that are produced beyond a function are known as global variables. Global variables should be used by everyone, both inside and outside of methods.

If you create a variable with the same name inside a feature, it will be local, which means it will only exist inside that function. The same-named global variable would remain global or have a similar meaning as before.

The global keywords:

A variable generated inside a feature is generally local, implying it can always be retrieved inside that function.

Within a function, a global keyword can be used to create a global variable.

The global keyword is used to change a global variable inside a function.

Assigning values to Variables in Python

As you can see from the preceding example, you will use an assignment operator = to allocate a value to a variable in Python.

Example 1: Declaring and assigning value to a variable

```
website = "apple.com"
print(website)
```

Output:

The variable website was given the value apple.com in the above program. The value allocated to the website, i.e. apple.com, was then printed out.

```
apple.com
```

Example 2: Changing the value of a variable

```
website = "apple.com"
print(website)

# assigning a new value to website
website = "programiz.com"

print(website)
```

Output:

```
apple.com
programiz.com
```

Initially, its website variable in the above program was set to apple.com. After that, the value is set to programiz.com.

Example 3: Assigning multiple values to multiple variables

We may accomplish this as follows if we wish to set the identical value to numerous variables at the same time:

```
a, b, c = 5, 3.2, "Hello"

print (a)
print (b)
print (c)
```

In the second program, the 3 variables x, y, and z are all given the identical string.

```
x = y = z = "same"

print (x)
print (y)
print (z)
```

2.5 Constants

The constant is a sort of variable that has a fixed value. Constants may be thought of as containers that carry information that cannot be modified later.

Constants might be thought of as a bag in which to keep certain books that cannot be replaced once put inside.

Assigning value to constant in Python

Constants are commonly defined and allocated in a module in Python. The module is a new file that contains variables, functions, and other information that is imported into the main file. Constants are typed in all upper case letters inside the module, with underscores between the terms.

Example 3: Declaring and assigning value to a constant

Create a constant.py:

```
PI = 3.14
GRAVITY = 9.8
```

Create a main.py:

```
import constant

print(constant.PI)
print(constant.GRAVITY)
```

Output:

```
3.14
9.8
```

We build a constant.py module directory in the preceding application. The constant value is then assigned to PI and GRAVITY. The constant module is then imported and a main.py file is created. Finally, the constant value is printed.

Chapter 3: Machine learning

Machine Learning is the process of teaching a computer to learn from data and statistics.

Machine Learning is the first step toward artificial intelligence (AI).

Software that evaluates data and attempts to anticipate the result is known as machine learning.

Set of data

A data set is actually the collection of data in a computer's thinking. It might be everything from a simple array to a whole database.

An array may be shown as follows:

```
[99,86,87,88,111,86,103,87,94,78,77,85,86]
```

The following is an example of the database:

Carname	Color	Age	Speed	AutoPass
BMW	red	5	99	Y
Volvo	black	7	86	Y
VW	gray	8	87	N
VW	white	7	88	Y
Ford	white	2	111	Y
VW	white	17	86	Y
Tesla	red	2	103	Y
BMW	black	9	87	Y
Volvo	gray	4	94	N
Ford	white	11	78	N
Toyota	gray	12	77	N
VW	white	9	85	N
Toyota	blue	6	86	Y

We can assume that the average number is approximately 80 or 90 by checking at the array, and we can also figure out the greatest and lowest values, but what more can we do?

And we can see from the information that white is the most frequent color and the oldest vehicle is 17 years old, so what if we can determine if a vehicle had an AutoPass just by checking through the other values?

That is the purpose of Machine Learning! Analyzing data and making predictions!

Types of Data

It's crucial to understand what kind of data we're working with before we can evaluate it.

The data types may be divided into three categories:

- Numerical
- Categorical
- Ordinal

Numerical:

Numbers are numerical data, which may be divided into two numeric categories:

1. Data That Isn't Continuous (Discrete Data)

The numbers can only be expressed as integers. The number of automobiles going past, for example.

2. Data that is constantly updated (Continuous Data)

The integers with an unlimited number of possibilities. For instance, the cost of an item and the size of the item

Categorical:

Categorical data is a set of values which cannot be compared to one another. A color value, for example, or any no/yes values.

Ordinal:

Ordinal data are similar to categorical data, but they may be compared. For instance, at school, an A is preferable to a B, and so on.

Knowing what sort of data your data source contains can help you choose which methodology to apply while studying it.

3.1 Mean, Median, and Mode

What can we understand from a group of digits/numbers?

There are three values that we are interested in when it comes to Machine Learning (and in mathematics):

Mean - The average value

Median - The midpoint value

Mode - The most common value

For instance, we've recorded the following speeds for 13 vehicles:

```
speed = [99,86,87,88,111,86,103,87,94,78,77,85,86]
```

What is the speed's average, median, or most common value?

Mean

The mean value is called the average value.

To obtain the mean, add all of the values together and divide by several values:

```
(99+86+87+88+111+86+103+87+94+78+77+85+86) / 13 = 89.77
```

As an example:

To obtain the average speed, use a NumPy mean() method:

```
import numpy

speed = [99,86,87,88,111,86,103,87,94,78,77,85,86]

x = numpy.mean(speed)

print(x)
```

Median

After you've sorted all of the data, a median value is one value in the middle:

Before you can determine the median, you must first sort the data.

77, 78, 85, 86, 86, 86, 87, 87, 88, 94, 99, 103, 111

As an example:

```
import numpy

speed = [99,86,87,88,111,86,103,87,94,78,77,85,86]

x = numpy.median(speed)

print(x)
```

To determine the center value, use a NumPy median() method:

Divide the total of the numbers in middle by two since there are two numbers in the center.

$$77, \ 78, \ 85, \ 86, \ 86, \ \underline{86, \ 87}, \ 87, \ 94, \ 98, \ 99, \ 103$$

$$(86 + 87) \ / \ 2 = \underline{86.5}$$

As an example:

Using a NumPy module:

```
import numpy

speed = [99,86,87,88,86,103,87,94,78,77,85,86]

x = numpy.median(speed)

print(x)
```

Mode

The value that occurs the most times is called the Mode value:

$$99, \ \underline{86}, \ 87, \ 88, \ 111, \ \underline{86}, \ 103, \ 87, \ 94, \ 78, \ 77, \ 85, \ \underline{86} = 86$$

As an example:

To discover the number that occurs the most, use a SciPy mode() method:

```
from scipy import stats

speed = [99,86,87,88,111,86,103,87,94,78,77,85,86]

x = stats.mode(speed)

print(x)
```

Each Mean, Median, and Mode are approaches that are frequently used in Machine Learning, therefore understanding the notion behind them is essential.

What is Standard Deviation?

The standard deviation is simply a number that expresses how far the data are spread out.

The low standard deviation indicates that the majority of the data points are near to the mean (average).

The numbers are spread out across a larger range when the standard deviation is high.

Consider the following scenario:

This time, we recorded the speeds of seven vehicles:

```
speed = [86,87,88,86,87,85,86]
```

A standard deviation is the following:

```
0.9
```

Meaning that the majority of values are within 0.9 of the mean value of 86.4.

Let's try the same thing with a broader range of numbers:

```
speed = [32,111,138,28,59,77,97]
```

A standard deviation is the following:

Meaning that the majority of values are within 37.85 of the mean value of 77.4.

As you can see, a greater standard deviation means the numbers are spread out across a larger range.

The standard deviation may be calculated using the NumPy module:

As an example:

To calculate the standard deviation, use a NumPy std() method:

```
import numpy

speed = [86,87,88,86,87,85,86]

x = numpy.std(speed)

print(x)
```

As an example:

Example:

```
import numpy

speed = [32,111,138,28,59,77,97]

x = numpy.std(speed)

print(x)
```

3.2 Variance

Another statistic that illustrates how evenly distributed the numbers are is variance.

In reality, the standard deviation may be calculated by taking a square root of a variance!

Alternatively, you may obtain the variance by multiplying a standard deviation by itself!

To determine the variance, perform these steps:

1. Calculate the mean.

$$(32+111+138+28+59+77+97) / 7 = 77.4$$

2. Calculate the difference from the mean for each value.

```
 32 - 77.4 = -45.4
111 - 77.4 =  33.6
138 - 77.4 =  60.6
 28 - 77.4 = -49.4
 59 - 77.4 = -18.4
 77 - 77.4 = - 0.4
 97 - 77.4 =  19.6
```

3. Determine the square value for each difference.

$$(-45.4)^2 = 2061.16$$
$$(33.6)^2 = 1128.96$$
$$(60.6)^2 = 3672.36$$
$$(-49.4)^2 = 2440.36$$
$$(-18.4)^2 = 338.56$$
$$(- 0.4)^2 = 0.16$$
$$(19.6)^2 = 384.16$$

4. An average number of such squared differences in the variance.

$$(2061.16+1128.96+3672.36+2440.36+338.56+0.16+384.16) / 7 = 1432.2$$

Fortunately, NumPy has such a method for calculating variance:

As an example:

```
import numpy

speed = [32,111,138,28,59,77,97]

x = numpy.var(speed)

print(x)
```

To get the variance, use a NumPy var() method:

3.3 Standard Deviation

As we've seen, each standard deviation is calculated by taking a square root of a variance:

$$\sqrt{1432.25} = 37.85$$

Use NumPy to compute the standard deviation, as in the previous example:

As an example:

To calculate the standard deviation, use a NumPy std() method:

```
import numpy

speed = [32,111,138,28,59,77,97]

x = numpy.std(speed)

print(x)
```

Symbols

The symbol Sigma σ is often used to denote standard deviation.

A symbol Sigma Square σ2 is often used to denote variance.

3.4 What Are Percentiles?

Percentiles are numbers for use in statistics to represent the value that a certain percent of values are less than.

Consider the following scenario: Let's imagine we have a list of all the ages of everyone who lives on a street.

```
ages = [5,31,43,48,50,41,7,11,15,39,80,82,32,2,8,6,25,36,27,61,31]
```

What percentage of the population is in the 75th percentile? The result is 43, indicating that 75percent of the total of population is aged 43 or younger.

A method for getting the given percentile is available in the NumPy module:

As an Example:

To get the percentiles, use a NumPy percentile() method:

```
import numpy

ages = [5,31,43,48,50,41,7,11,15,39,80,82,32,2,8,6,25,36,27,61,31]

x = numpy.percentile(ages, 75)

print(x)
```

As an Example:

And what's the age at which 90% of the population is younger?

```
import numpy

ages = [5,31,43,48,50,41,7,11,15,39,80,82,32,2,8,6,25,36,27,61,31]

x = numpy.percentile(ages, 90)

print(x)
```

3.5 Data Distribution

We used extremely tiny amounts of information in our examples earlier in this course to help us comprehend the various concepts.

The data sets in the actual world are substantially larger, yet gathering real data of the world, at least at the beginning of a project, may be challenging.

How do we obtain big data sets?

We utilize the Python package NumPy to generate large data sets in testing, which has a variety of techniques for generating random data sets of arbitrary size.

Example:

Make an array of 250 random floats in the range of 0 to 5:

```
import numpy

x = numpy.random.uniform(0.0, 5.0, 250)

print(x)
```

Histogram:

We can use the data we obtained to create a histogram to display the data set.

To create a histogram, we'll utilize the Python program Matplotlib.

Example

Create/Draw a histogram:

```
import numpy
import matplotlib.pyplot as plt

x = numpy.random.uniform(0.0, 5.0, 250)

plt.hist(x, 5)
plt.show()
```

Answer:

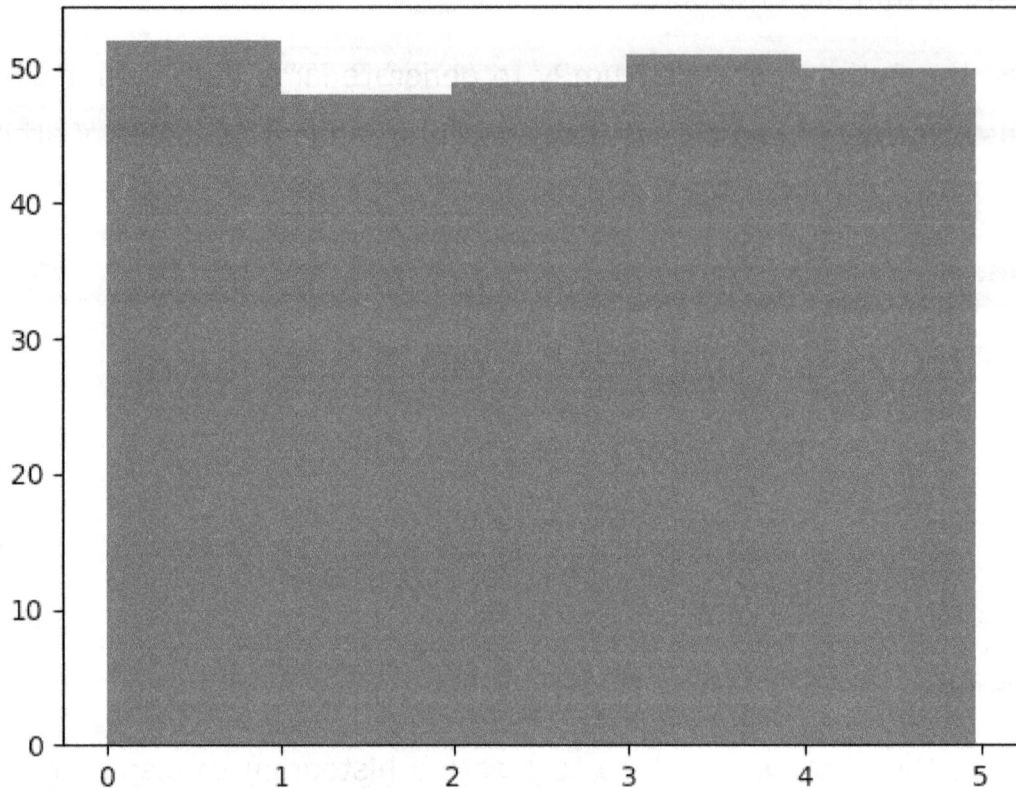

Histogram Explaination:

We create a histogram having 5 bars using an array from the previous example.

The first bar indicates the number of items in the array that are within 0 and 1.

The second bar depicts the number of values that fall within 1 and 2.

And so forth.

As a consequence, we get the following:

There are 52 values within 0 and 1

There are 48 values within 1 and 2

There are 49 values within 2 and 3

There are 51 values within 3 and 4

There are 50 values within 4 and 5

Big Data Distributions

Although a data set of 250 numbers is not regarded as large, now that you know how to produce a random collection of values, you may make a data set as large as you like by modifying the settings.

As an example:

Create an array of 100000 random integers and use a histogram having 100 bars to represent them:

```python
import numpy
import matplotlib.pyplot as plt


x = numpy.random.uniform(0.0, 5.0, 100000)


plt.hist(x, 100)
plt.show()
```

3.6 Normal Data Distribution

We learned how to create a random array of a certain size and between two specified values in the previous chapter.

We'll learn how to make an array with values centered around a single item in this chapter.

This type of data distribution is known in probability theory as the Gaussian data distribution or the normal data distribution, just after mathematician Carl Friedrich Gauss, who devised the formula for it.

As an example:

A basic normal data distribution looks like this:

```python
import numpy
import matplotlib.pyplot as plt

x = numpy.random.normal(5.0, 1.0, 100000)

plt.hist(x, 100)
plt.show()
```

Result:

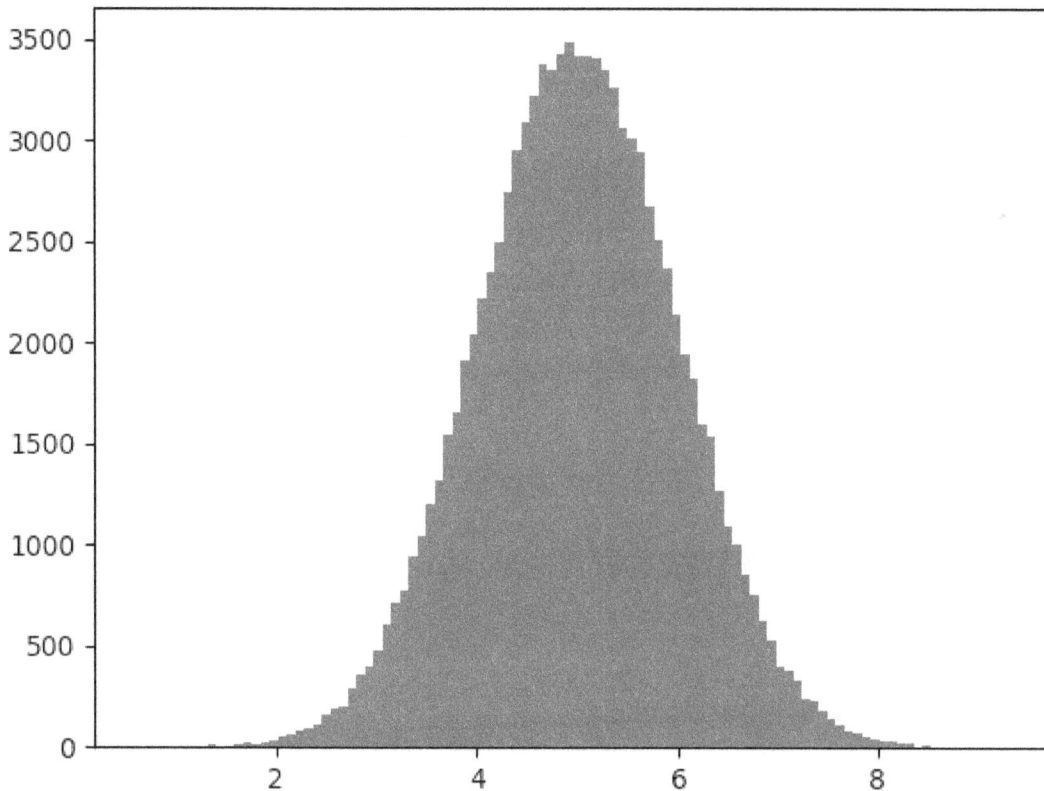

Histogram Explaination:

To construct a histogram with 100 bars, we utilize the array returned by the numpy.random.normal() function, which has 100000 values.

The mean value is set to 5.0, while a standard deviation is set to 1.0.

This means that the results should be clustered around 5.0 and seldom deviate from the mean by more than 1.0.

As you can observe from the histogram, the majority of the values are somewhere within 4.0 and 6.0, with a peak around 5.0.

3.7 Scatter Plot

The scatter plot is a graph in which each data point is symbolized by a dot.

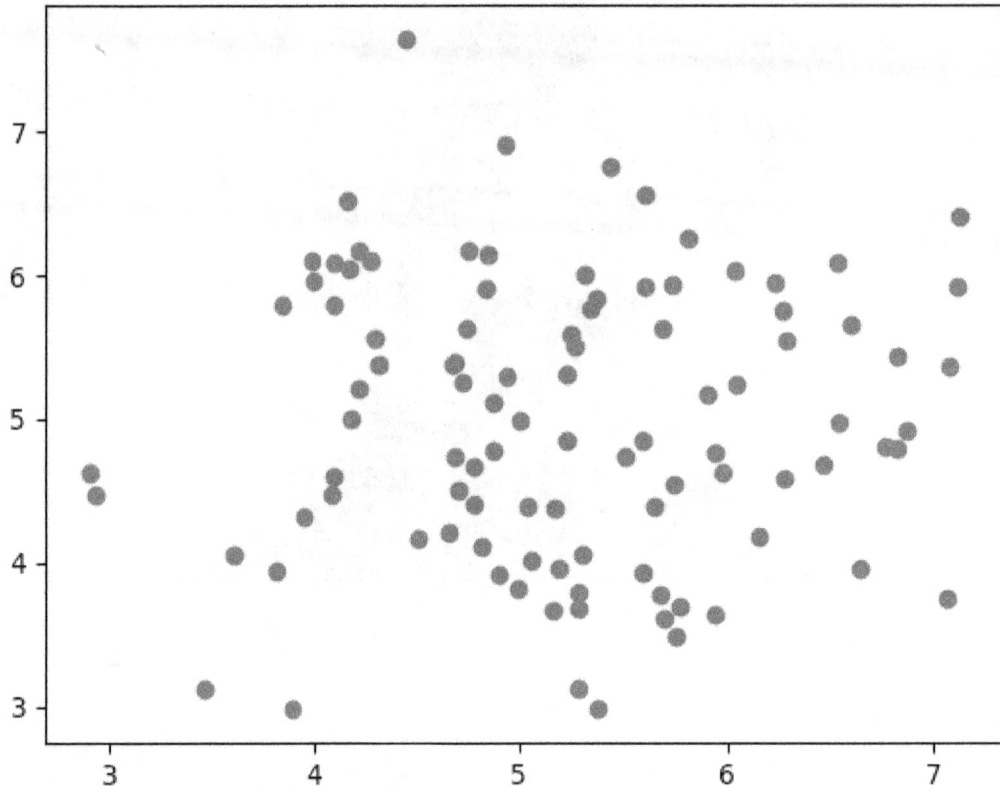

The Matplotlib module offers a method for producing scatter plots that require two identical-length arrays, one for the x-axis values and the other for the y-axis data:

```
x = [5,7,8,7,2,17,2,9,4,11,12,9,6]

y = [99,86,87,88,111,86,103,87,94,78,77,85,86]
```

Each car's age is represented by the x array.

Each car's speed is represented by the y array.

Example:

To create a scatter plot diagram, use the scatter() method:

```
import matplotlib.pyplot as plt

x = [5,7,8,7,2,17,2,9,4,11,12,9,6]
y = [99,86,87,88,111,86,103,87,94,78,77,85,86]

plt.scatter(x, y)
plt.show()
```

Result:

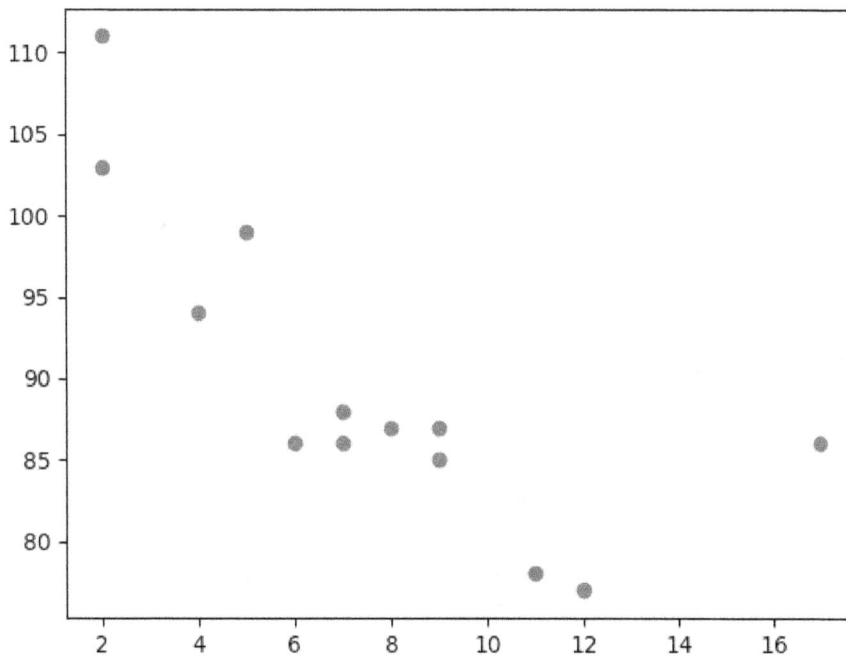

Scatter Plot Explanation:

The ages are shown on the x-axis, while the speeds are shown on the y-axis.

172

The graphic shows that the two quickest automobiles were both two years old, while the slowest vehicle was twelve years old.

3.8 Random Data Distributions

The data sets in Machine Learning may include hundreds, if not millions, of variables.

When assessing an algorithm, you may need to utilize randomly generated values if you don't have real-world data.

The NumPy module may assist us with that, as we learned in the last chapter!

Let's make two arrays, each containing 1000 random integers drawn from a normal distribution of data.

The mean of the first array will be fixed to 5.0, with a standard deviation of 1.0.

The mean of the second array will be set to 10.0, with the standard deviation of 2.0:

Example:

The scatter plot having 1000 dots:

```
import numpy
import matplotlib.pyplot as plt

x = numpy.random.normal(5.0, 1.0, 1000)
y = numpy.random.normal(10.0, 2.0, 1000)

plt.scatter(x, y)
plt.show()
```

Result:

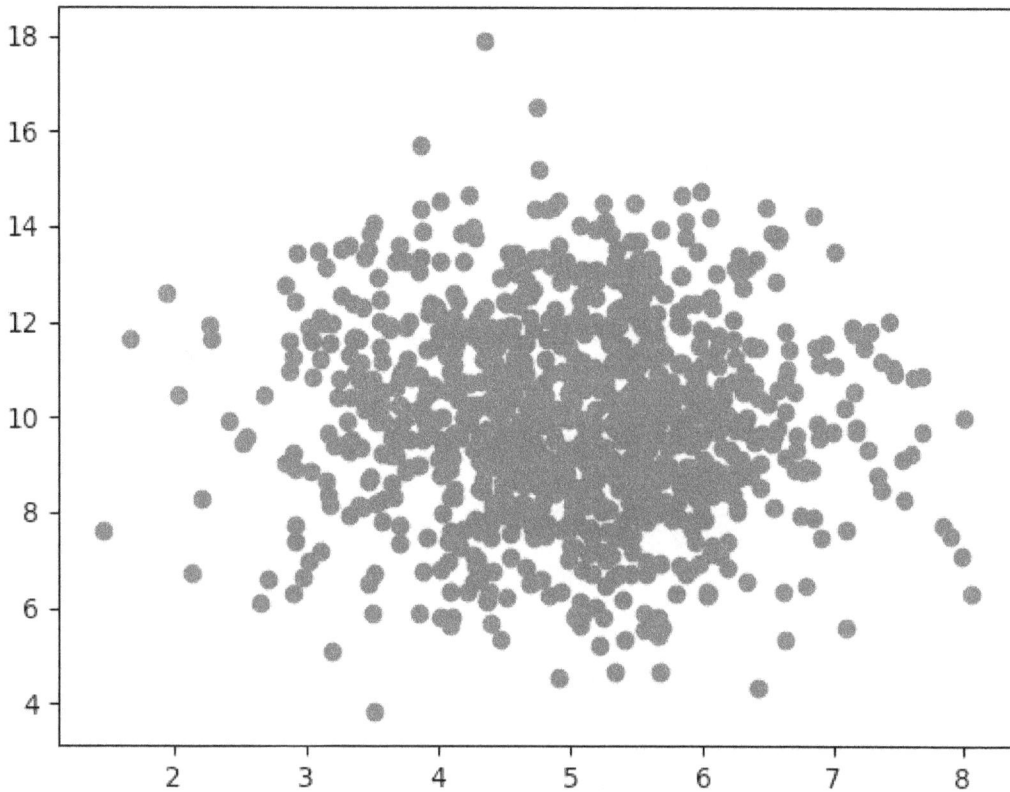

Scatter Plot Explanation:

On the x-axis, all dots seem concentrated around a value of 5; on the y-axis, each dot seem concentrated around a value of 10.

On the y-axis, we can also observe that the dispersion is larger than that on the x-axis.

Regression

When attempting to determine the connection between variables, the word regression is utilized.

That connection is applied to determine the outcome of upcoming occurrences in Machine Learning and statistical modeling.

3.9 Linear Regression

Linear regression draws a straight line across all of the data points based on their connection.

This line may be used to forecast values in the future.

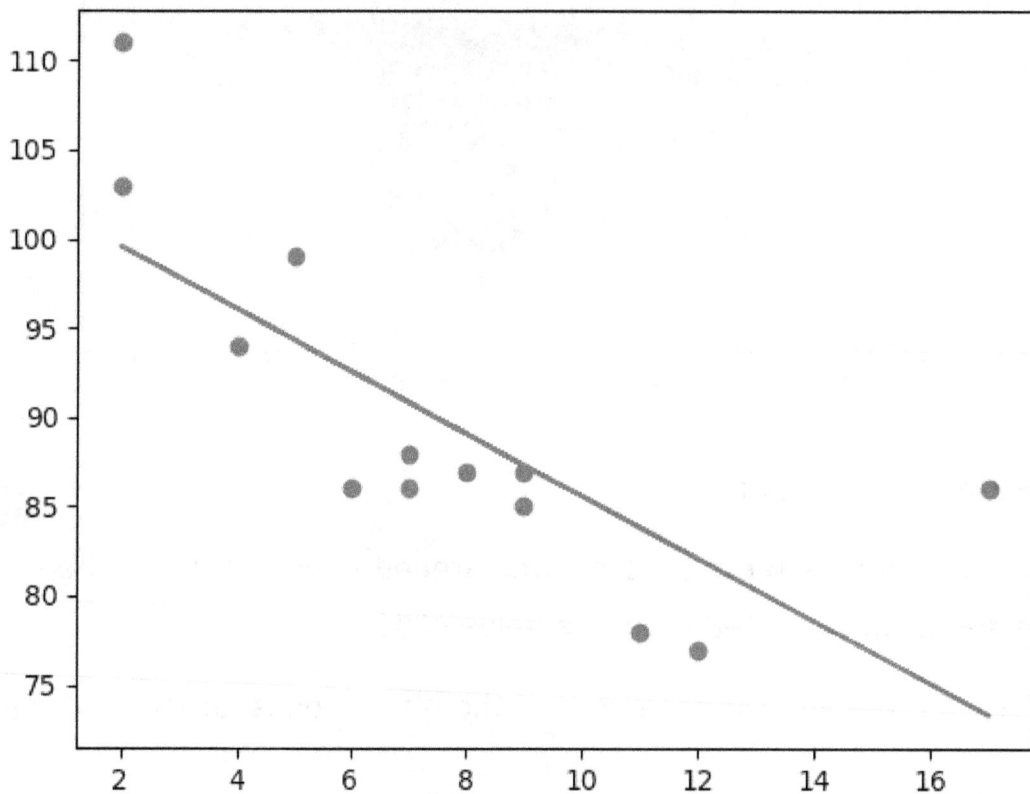

Predicting the next is crucial in Machine Learning.

Working of linear regression?

Python has functions for determining a link between data points and drawing a linear regression line. Instead of going over the mathematical formula, we'll teach you how to apply these strategies.

The x-axis indicates age, while the y-axis indicates the speed in the example below. We recorded the speed and age13 vehicles as they passed through a tollbooth. Let's see whether we can utilize the data we gathered inside a linear regression:

Example:

To begin, create a scatter plot as follows:

```
import matplotlib.pyplot as plt

x = [5,7,8,7,2,17,2,9,4,11,12,9,6]
y = [99,86,87,88,111,86,103,87,94,78,77,85,86]

plt.scatter(x, y)
plt.show()
```

Result:

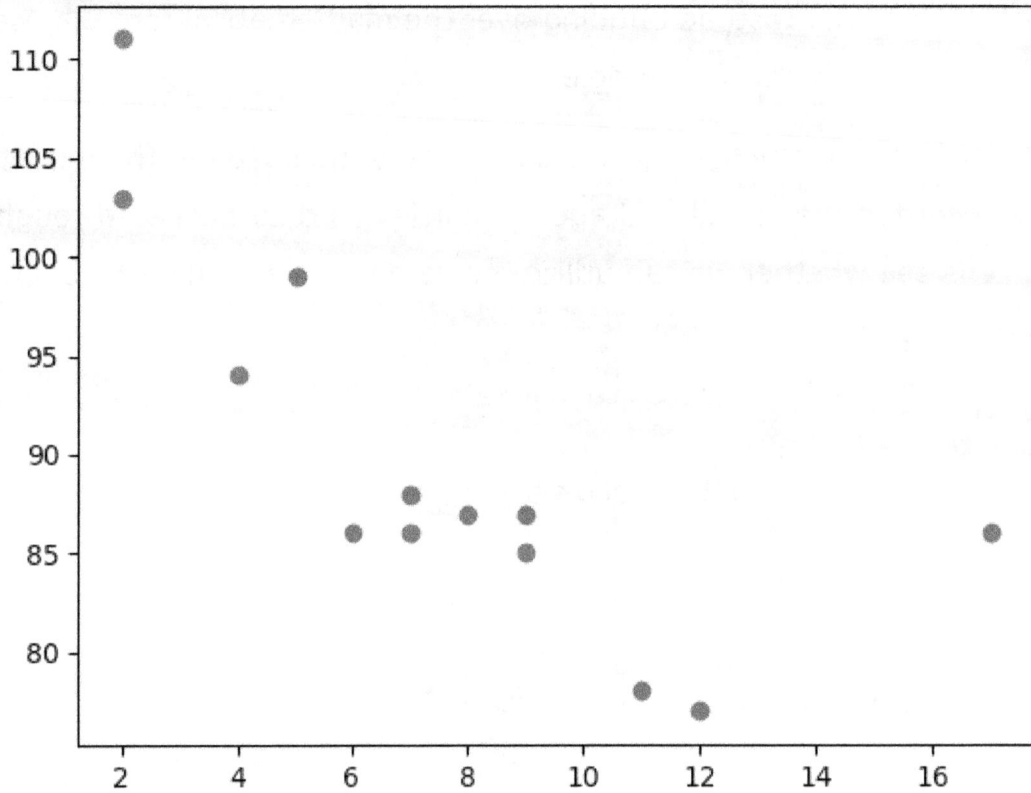

Example:

Import scipy and construct a Linear Regression line:

```
import matplotlib.pyplot as plt
from scipy import stats

x = [5,7,8,7,2,17,2,9,4,11,12,9,6]
y = [99,86,87,88,111,86,103,87,94,78,77,85,86]

slope, intercept, r, p, std_err = stats.linregress(x, y)

def myfunc(x):
  return slope * x + intercept

mymodel = list(map(myfunc, x))

plt.scatter(x, y)
plt.plot(x, mymodel)
plt.show()
```

Result:

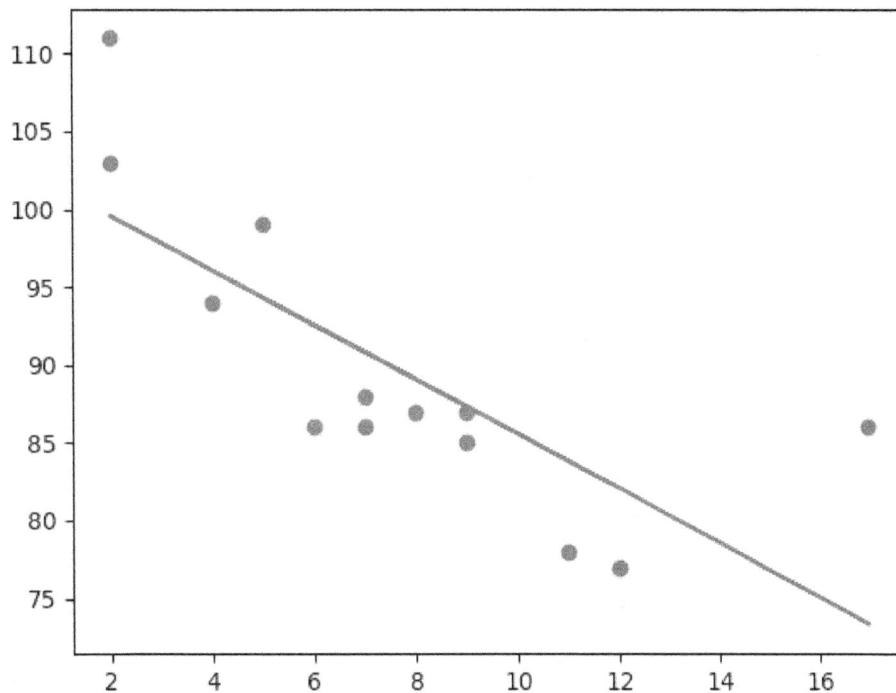

Example Explaination:

Import the modules that you need.

```
import matplotlib.pyplot as plt
from scipy import stats
```

Make the following arrays to represent the y and x axis values:

```
x = [5,7,8,7,2,17,2,9,4,11,12,9,6]
y = [99,86,87,88,111,86,103,87,94,78,77,85,86]
```

Run the method that returns certain critical Linear Regression key values:

```
slope, intercept, r, p, std_err = stats.linregress(x, y)
```

Initialize a function that returns a new value based on the intercept and slope variables. This new value indicates where the relevant x value will now be put on the y-axis:

```
def myfunc(x):
    return slope * x + intercept
```

Run the function on each value in the x array. As a consequence, a unique array with new y-axis values will be created:

```
mymodel = list(map(myfunc, x))
```

Create an original scatter plot as follows:

```
plt.scatter(x, y)
```

Draw the linear regression line as follows:

```
plt.plot(x, mymodel)
```

Display the diagram as follows:

```
plt.show()
```

R stands for Relationship

It's crucial to understand the link between the values on the y-axis and the values on the x-axis; if there isn't one; linear regression won't be able to predict anything.

The coefficient of correlation, or r, is the name given to this connection.

An r value ranges between -1 to 1, with 0 indicating no association and 1 and -1 indicating 100% association.

Simply you have to do is supply the x and y numbers to the Scipy and Python module, and it will calculate the result for you.

Example:

In a linear regression, how effectively does my data fit?

```
from scipy import stats

x = [5,7,8,7,2,17,2,9,4,11,12,9,6]
y = [99,86,87,88,111,86,103,87,94,78,77,85,86]

slope, intercept, r, p, std_err = stats.linregress(x, y)

print(r)
```

Predict Future Values

We can now utilize the data we've obtained to forecast future values.

Example: Let's say you're trying to forecast the overall speed of a ten-year-old automobile.

To accomplish so, we'll use the same myfunc() method as in the previous example:

```
def myfunc(x):
    return slope * x + intercept
```

Example:

Estimate the approximate speed of a ten-year-old automobile:

```
from scipy import stats

x = [5,7,8,7,2,17,2,9,4,11,12,9,6]
y = [99,86,87,88,111,86,103,87,94,78,77,85,86]

slope, intercept, r, p, std_err = stats.linregress(x, y)

def myfunc(x):
    return slope * x + intercept

speed = myfunc(10)

print(speed)
```

The example projected an 85.6 mph speed, which we could also see in the diagram:

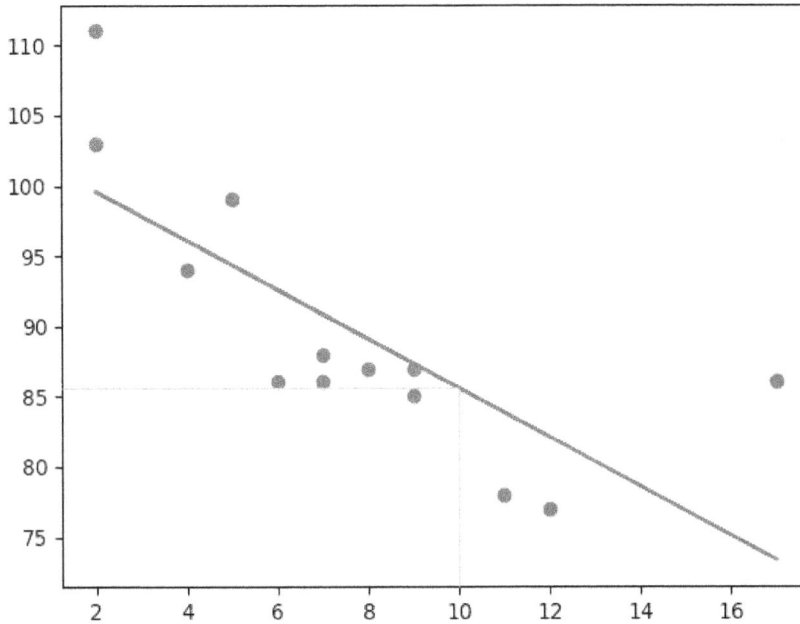

Bad Fit?

Let's imagine a situation where linear regression isn't the optimal strategy for predicting future values.

Example:

These x- and y-axis values should lead to a poor fit for linear regression:

```python
import matplotlib.pyplot as plt
from scipy import stats

x = [89,43,36,36,95,10,66,34,38,20,26,29,48,64,6,5,36,66,72,40]
y = [21,46,3,35,67,95,53,72,58,10,26,34,90,33,38,20,56,2,47,15]

slope, intercept, r, p, std_err = stats.linregress(x, y)

def myfunc(x):
  return slope * x + intercept

mymodel = list(map(myfunc, x))

plt.scatter(x, y)
plt.plot(x, mymodel)
plt.show()
```

Result:

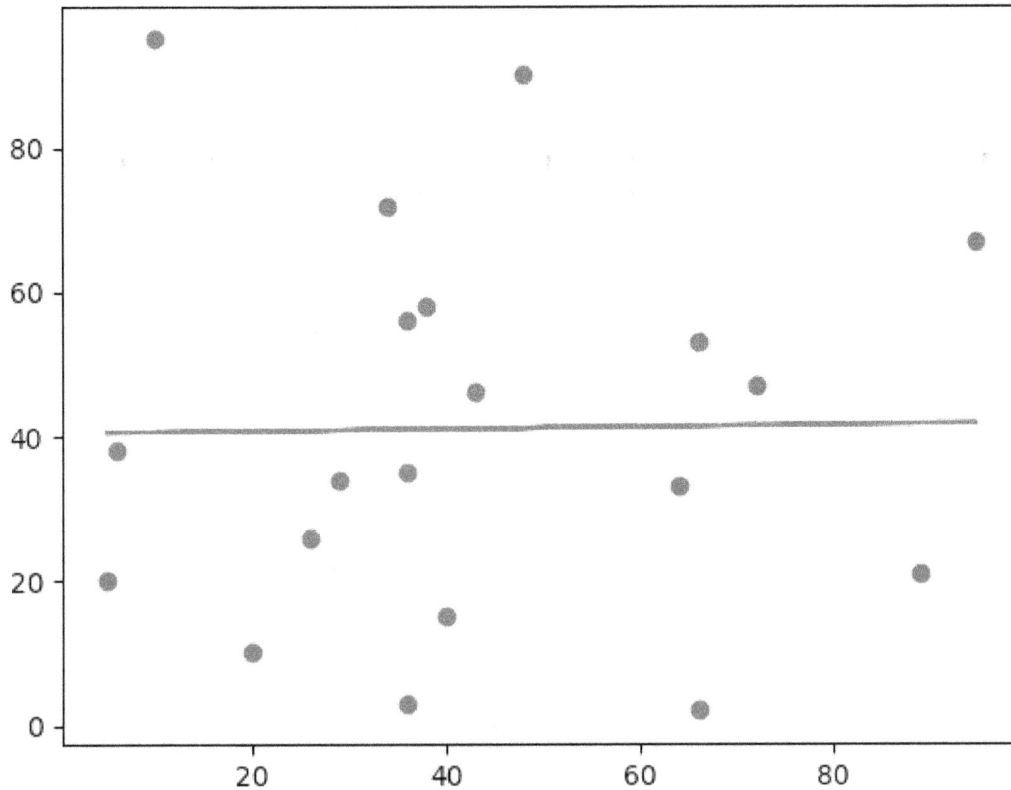

And what about the r in a relationship?

Example:

The r value should be quite low.

```
import numpy
from scipy import stats


x = [89,43,36,36,95,10,66,34,38,20,26,29,48,64,6,5,36,66,72,40]
y = [21,46,3,35,67,95,53,72,58,10,26,34,90,33,38,20,56,2,47,15]

slope, intercept, r, p, std_err = stats.linregress(x, y)

print(r)
```

The result: 0.013 denotes a poor association and suggests that this data set is unsuitable for linear regression.

3.10 Polynomial Regression

If your data points do not match the linear regression which is a straight line connecting all data points), polynomial regression may be the best option.

Polynomial regression, similar to linear regression, looks for the optimum method to draw a line across the data points based on the connection among the variables x and y.

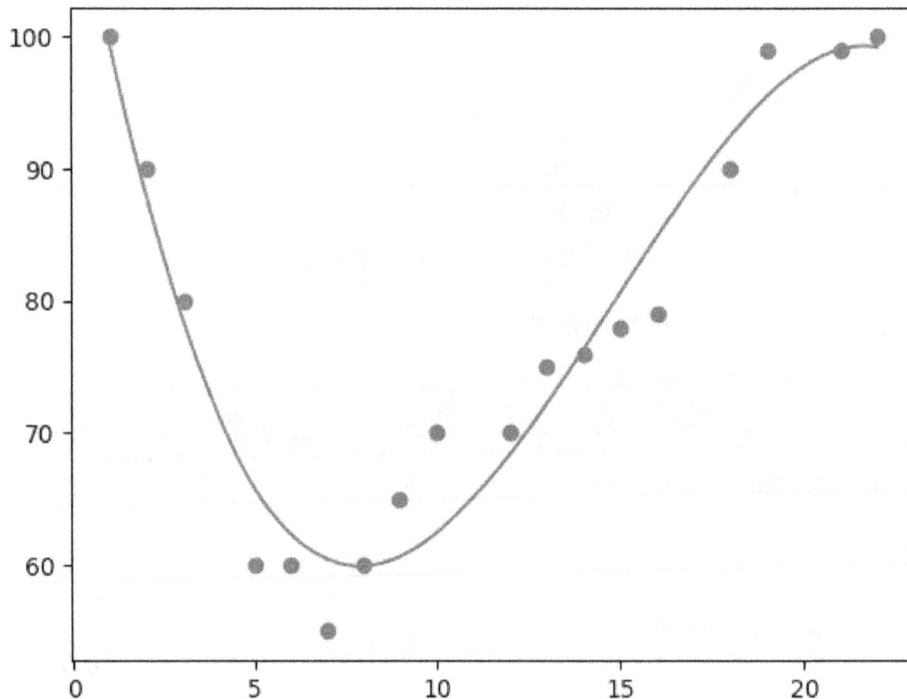

Working of polynomial regression:

Python has functions for determining a link between data points and drawing a polynomial regression line. Instead of going over the mathematical formula, we'll teach you how to apply these strategies.

In the example below, 18 automobiles were recorded as they passed through a tollbooth.

We recorded the car's speed as well as a time of day hour when it passed us.

All hours of a day are shown on the x-axis, while the speed is shown on the y-axis:

Example:

To begin, create a scatter plot as follows:

```python
import matplotlib.pyplot as plt

x = [1,2,3,5,6,7,8,9,10,12,13,14,15,16,18,19,21,22]
y = [100,90,80,60,60,55,60,65,70,70,75,76,78,79,90,99,99,100]

plt.scatter(x, y)
plt.show()
```

Result:

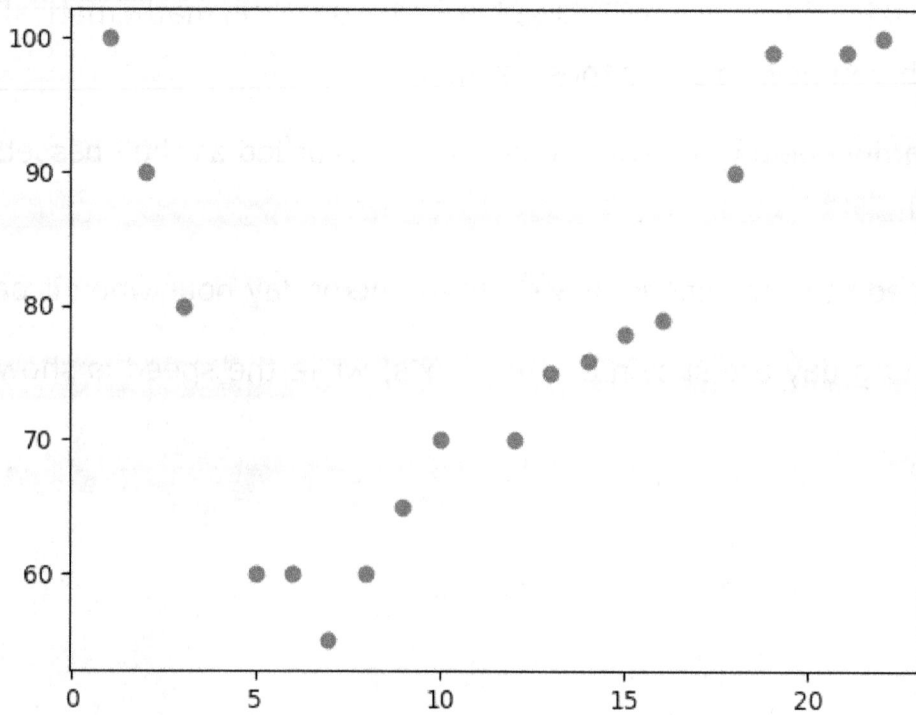

Example:

Import numpy and matplotlib, then draw the Polynomial Regression line as follows:

```
import numpy
import matplotlib.pyplot as plt

x = [1,2,3,5,6,7,8,9,10,12,13,14,15,16,18,19,21,22]
y = [100,90,80,60,60,55,60,65,70,70,75,76,78,79,90,99,99,100]

mymodel = numpy.poly1d(numpy.polyfit(x, y, 3))

myline = numpy.linspace(1, 22, 100)

plt.scatter(x, y)
plt.plot(myline, mymodel(myline))
plt.show()
```

Result:

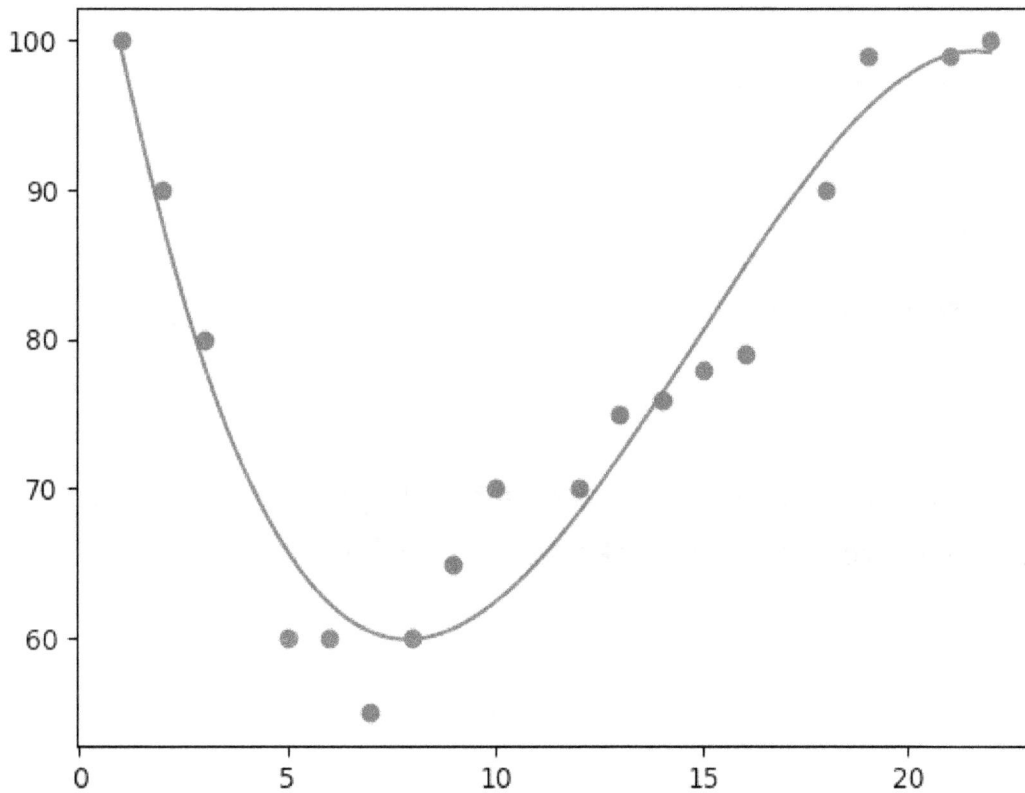

R-Squared

It is critical to understand how strongly the x- and y-axis values are related; if there is no link, polynomial regression cannot be utilized to forecast anything.

The r-squared number is used to assess the connection.

The r-squared value varies from 0 to 1, with 0 indicating no association and 1 indicating 100% connection.

This value will be computed for you by Python using the Sklearn module; all you must do is provide it the y and x arrays:

Example:

In a polynomial regression, how well does my data fit?

```python
import numpy
from sklearn.metrics import r2_score

x = [1,2,3,5,6,7,8,9,10,12,13,14,15,16,18,19,21,22]
y = [100,90,80,60,60,55,60,65,70,70,75,76,78,79,90,99,99,100]

mymodel = numpy.poly1d(numpy.polyfit(x, y, 3))

print(r2_score(y, mymodel(x)))
```

Note: The 0.94 indicates that the association is quite strong, and we may utilize polynomial regression to make future predictions.

3.11 Multiple Regression

Multiple regression is similar to linear regression, but it includes upwards of one independent value, implying that we are attempting to predict a value using two or more factors.

We can forecast a car's CO_2 emissions based on its engine size, but multiple regression allows us to include extra factors, such as the car's weight, to improve the accuracy of the forecast.

Working of multiple regression:

We have modules in Python that will perform the job for us. To begin, import the Pandas module.

We can scan csv files then return the DataFrame object using the Pandas module.

After that, build a list of independent values and label it X.

Create a variable named y to hold the dependent values.

Each list of independent variables is usually labeled with an upper case X, while a list of dependant values is labeled with a lower case y.

We'll need to import the sklearn module since we'll be using several of its methods.

To generate a linear regression object, we'll utilize the LinearRegression() function from the sklearn package.

Fit() is a method on this object that accepts as input all dependant and independent values then fills a regression object with data that specifies the connection.

We now have the regression object that can forecast CO2 levels based on the weight and volume of an automobile.

Example:

To see the entire example in action, go to:

```
import pandas
from sklearn import linear_model

df = pandas.read_csv("cars.csv")

X = df[['Weight', 'Volume']]
y = df['CO2']

regr = linear_model.LinearRegression()
regr.fit(X, y)

#predict the CO2 emission of a car where the weight is 2300kg, and the volume is 1300cm³:
predictedCO2 = regr.predict([[2300, 1300]])

print(predictedCO2)
```

Result:

```
[107.2087328]
```

An automobile with a 1.3 liter engine and a weight of 2300 kg would emit roughly 107 grams of CO_2 each kilometer driven, according to our calculations.

Coefficient

A coefficient is a number that represents the connection between two variables that are unknown.

Example: Assuming x is the variable, 2x is x multiplied by two. The number 2 represents the coefficient, while x is an unknown variable. In this scenario, we may inquire about the weight-to-CO2 coefficient and the volume-to-CO2 coefficient. The answer(s) we obtain inform us what will happen if either of the independent quantities is increased or decreased.

Example:

Print the regression object's coefficient values:

```
import pandas
from sklearn import linear_model

df = pandas.read_csv("cars.csv")

X = df[['Weight', 'Volume']]
y = df['CO2']

regr = linear_model.LinearRegression()
regr.fit(X, y)

print(regr.coef_)
```

Result:

```
[0.00755095 0.00780526]
```

3.12 Scale

Scale Features:

It might be challenging to compare data that has various values and even various measuring units. What is the difference between kilos and meters? Or how about altitude vs. time?

Scaling is the solution to this issue. We may change the size of the data to make it simpler to compare.

Comparing the volume 1.0 to the weight 790 might be tough, although if we scale those all into similar numbers, we can observe how much one number differs from the other.

Scaling data may be done in a variety of ways; in this lesson, we'll utilize a technique called standardization.

This formula is used in the standardization method:

```
z = (x - u) / s
```

Where z represents the new value, x represents the old value, u represents the mean, and s represents the standard deviation.

The first value as in the weight column from a data set above is 790, and a scaled value is:

```
(790 - 1292.23) / 238.74 = -2.1
```

The initial value in a volume column from all data set above is 1.0, so the scaled value is:

```
(1.0 - 1.61) / 0.38 = -1.59
```

Rather than comparing 790 to 1.0, you may instead compare -2.1 to -1.59.

A Python sklearn module contains a function called StandardScaler() that produces a Scaler object containing methods for altering data sets, so you don't have to do it manually.

Example:

All values throughout the Volume and Weight columns should be scaled as follows:

```python
import pandas
from sklearn import linear_model
from sklearn.preprocessing import StandardScaler
scale = StandardScaler()

df = pandas.read_csv("cars2.csv")

X = df[['Weight', 'Volume']]

scaledX = scale.fit_transform(X)

print(scaledX)
```

Result:

```
[[-2.10389253 -1.59336644]
 [-0.55407235 -1.07190106]
 [-1.52166278 -1.59336644]
 [-1.78973979 -1.85409913]
 [-0.63784641 -0.28970299]
 [-1.52166278 -1.59336644]
 [-0.76769621 -0.55043568]
 [ 0.3046118  -0.28970299]
 [-0.7551301  -0.28970299]
 [-0.59595938 -0.0289703 ]
 [-1.30803892 -1.33263375]
 [-1.26615189 -0.81116837]
 [-0.7551301  -1.59336644]
 [-0.16871166 -0.0289703 ]
 [ 0.14125238 -0.0289703 ]
 [ 0.15800719 -0.0289703 ]
 [ 0.3046118  -0.0289703 ]
 [-0.05142797  1.53542584]
 [-0.72580918 -0.0289703 ]
 [ 0.14962979  1.01396046]
 [ 1.2219378  -0.0289703 ]
 [ 0.5685001   1.01396046]
 [ 0.3046118   1.27469315]
 [ 0.51404696 -0.0289703 ]
 [ 0.51404696  1.01396046]
 [ 0.72348212 -0.28970299]
 [ 0.8281997   1.01396046]
 [ 1.81254495  1.01396046]
 [ 0.96642691 -0.0289703 ]
 [ 1.72877089  1.01396046]
 [ 1.30990057  1.27469315]
 [ 1.90050772  1.01396046]
 [-0.23991961 -0.0289703 ]
 [ 0.40932938 -0.0289703 ]
 [ 0.47215993 -0.0289703 ]
 [ 0.4302729   2.31762392]]
```

Predict CO2 Values

As in the Multiple Regression chapter, you had to forecast how much CO2 an automobile will emit based on its weight and volume.

You must utilize the scale when predicting values if a data set is scaled:

Example:

Calculate the CO2 emissions from a 2300 kilogram 1.3 liter car:

```python
import pandas
from sklearn import linear_model
from sklearn.preprocessing import StandardScaler
scale = StandardScaler()

df = pandas.read_csv("cars2.csv")

X = df[['Weight', 'Volume']]
y = df['CO2']

scaledX = scale.fit_transform(X)

regr = linear_model.LinearRegression()
regr.fit(scaledX, y)

scaled = scale.transform([[2300, 1.3]])

predictedCO2 = regr.predict([scaled[0]])
print(predictedCO2)
```

Result:

```
[107.2087328]
```

3.13 Train/ Test

Assess Your Model

In Machine Learning, we develop models to predict the result of certain events, such as the CO2 emissions of a vehicle based on its weight and engine size in the previous chapter.

We may use the Train/Test technique to see if a model is effective enough.

What is Train/Test?

Train/Test is a technique for determining your model's correctness.

Because you divide that data set across two sets named as a training set or a testing set, it's termed Train/Test.

Training accounts for 80% of the budget while testing accounts for 20%.

The training set is used to train the model.

The testing set is used to test the model.

The term "train the model" refers to the process of developing a model.

Testing the model entails determining its correctness.

Start With a Data Set

Begin by selecting a data set to test.

Our data set depicts the purchasing behavior of 100 clients at a store.

Example:

```
import numpy
import matplotlib.pyplot as plt
numpy.random.seed(2)

x = numpy.random.normal(3, 1, 100)
y = numpy.random.normal(150, 40, 100) / x

plt.scatter(x, y)
plt.show()
```

Result:

The duration of minutes before making a transaction is shown on the x-axis.

The amount paid on the purchase is shown on the y axis.

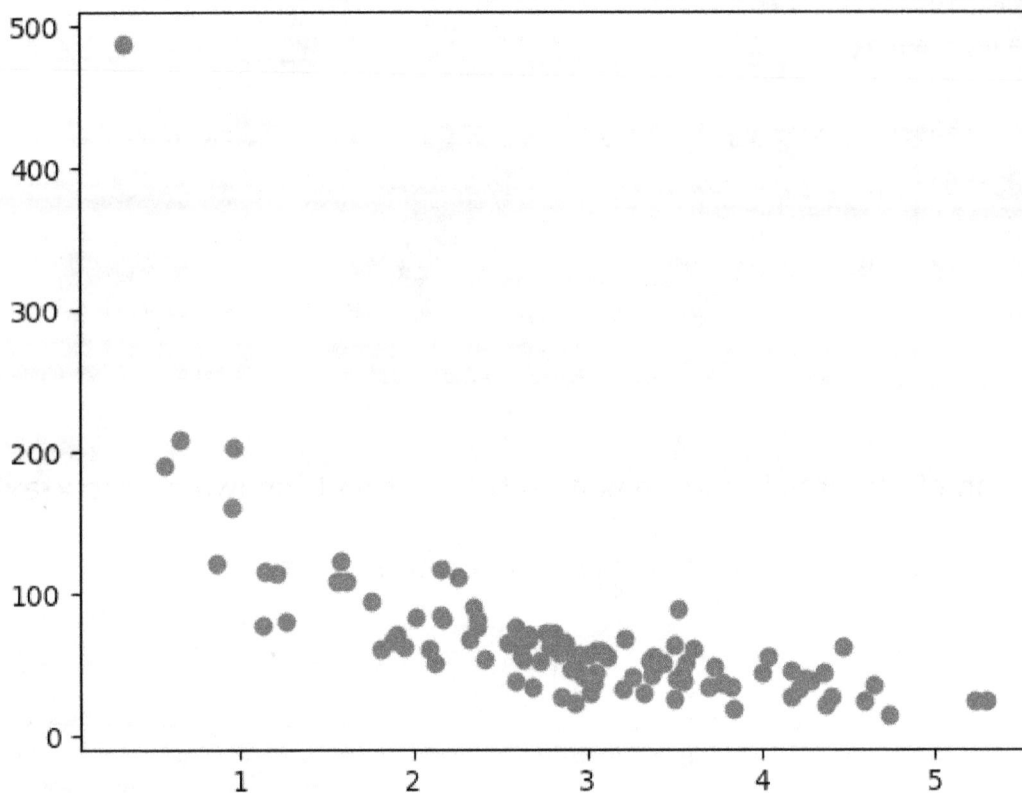

Split Into Train/Test

The random selection of over 80 percent of its total original data should be used as the training set.

The remaining 20% should be used for testing.

```
train_x = x[:80]
train_y = y[:80]

test_x = x[80:]
test_y = y[80:]
```

Display the Training Set

Display the training set's scatter plot as well:

Example:

```
plt.scatter(train_x, train_y)
plt.show()
```

Result:

It seems to be a good pick, as it appears to be the original data set:

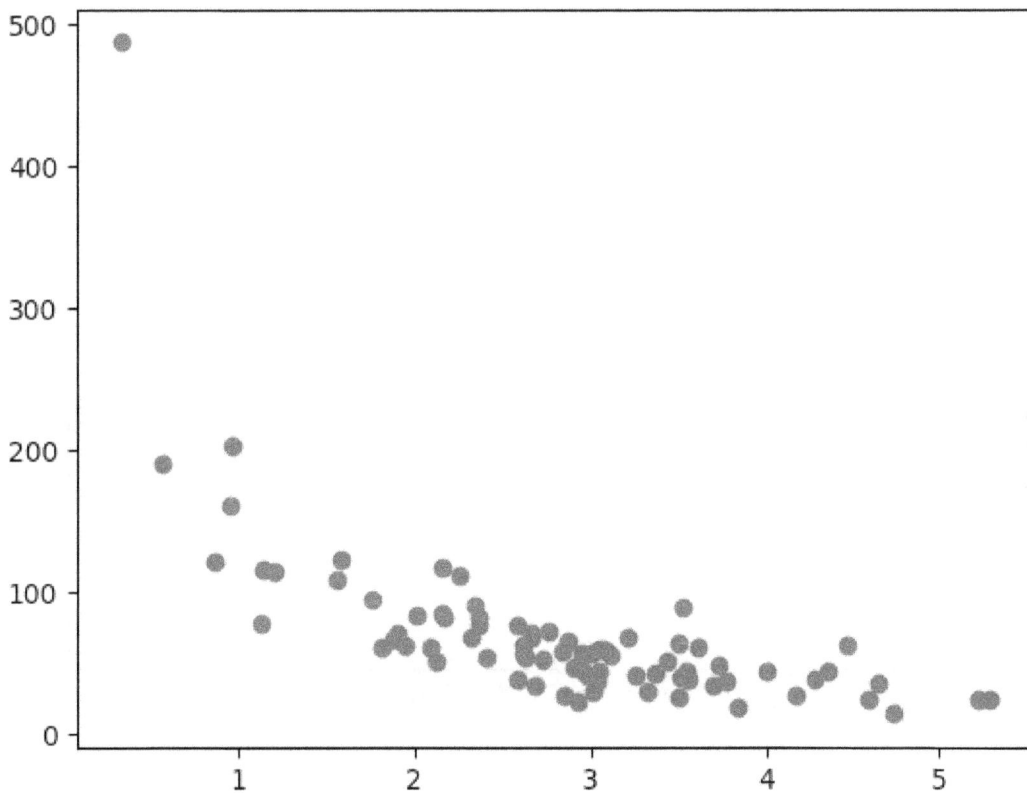

Display the Testing Set

We'll also look just at the testing set to make sure it's not radically different.

Example:

```
plt.scatter(test_x, test_y)
plt.show()
```

Result:

The testing set resembles an original data set in appearance:

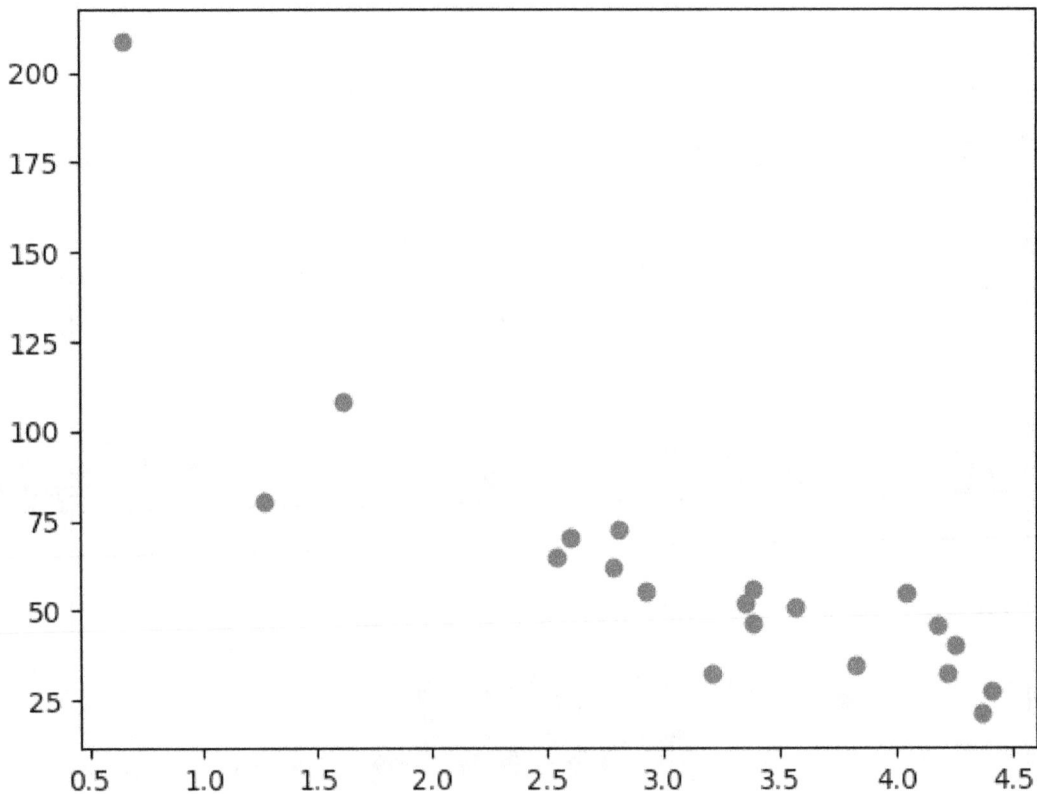

Fit the Data Set

How will the data set appear? A polynomial regression, in my view, would be the best match, therefore let's create a polynomial regression line.

The plot() function of a matplotlib module is used to create a line across the data points:

Example:

Connect the data points using a polynomial regression line:

```
import numpy
import matplotlib.pyplot as plt
numpy.random.seed(2)

x = numpy.random.normal(3, 1, 100)
y = numpy.random.normal(150, 40, 100) / x

train_x = x[:80]
train_y = y[:80]

test_x = x[80:]
test_y = y[80:]

mymodel = numpy.poly1d(numpy.polyfit(train_x, train_y, 4))

myline = numpy.linspace(0, 6, 100)

plt.scatter(train_x, train_y)
plt.plot(myline, mymodel(myline))
plt.show()
```

Result:

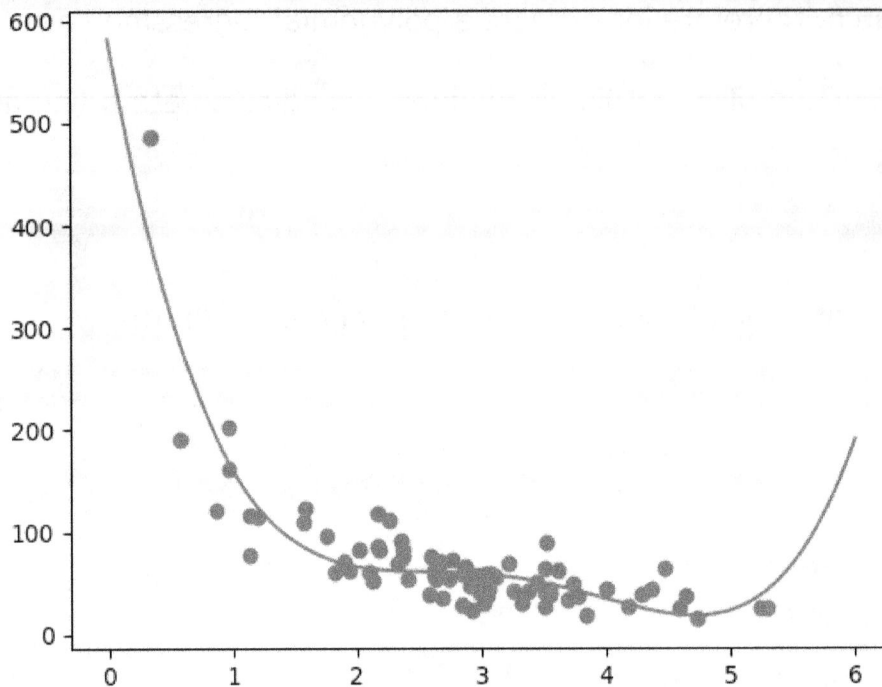

Even while it might give us some strange results if we tried to forecast values beyond the data set, the outcome supports my recommendation of fitting the data set to a polynomial regression. For example, the line suggests that a consumer who spends 6 minutes inside the store will spend $200. Overfitting is most likely the cause of this.

R2

R2, often known as R-squared, comes to mind?

It quantifies the connection between the x and y axes, with a value ranging from 0 to 1, with 0 indicating no connection and 1 indicating a complete connection.

The r2 score() function in the sklearn module will assist us in determining this connection.

In this situation, we'd want to see whether there's a link between the number of minutes a customer spends in the store and the amount of money they spend.

Example:

In a polynomial regression, how well would my training data fit?

The result of 0.799 indicates that the relationship is satisfactory ok.

```
import numpy
from sklearn.metrics import r2_score
numpy.random.seed(2)

x = numpy.random.normal(3, 1, 100)
y = numpy.random.normal(150, 40, 100) / x

train_x = x[:80]
train_y = y[:80]

test_x = x[80:]
test_y = y[80:]

mymodel = numpy.poly1d(numpy.polyfit(train_x, train_y, 4))

r2 = r2_score(train_y, mymodel(train_x))

print(r2)
```

Bring in the Testing Set

Now we have the acceptable model, at least in terms of training data.

We want to verify the model using the testing data to check whether it produces the same results.

Example:

Let's see how to calculate the R2 score while utilizing testing data:

204

```
import numpy
from sklearn.metrics import r2_score
numpy.random.seed(2)

x = numpy.random.normal(3, 1, 100)
y = numpy.random.normal(150, 40, 100) / x

train_x = x[:80]
train_y = y[:80]

test_x = x[80:]
test_y = y[80:]

mymodel = numpy.poly1d(numpy.polyfit(train_x, train_y, 4))

r2 = r2_score(test_y, mymodel(test_x))

print(r2)
```

The result of 0.809 indicates that the model also matches the testing set, and we are sure that we can use it to forecast future values.

Predict Values

We can start forecasting new values now that we've demonstrated that this model is valid.

Example:

How much will a shopping consumer spend if he or she spends 5 minutes in the store?

```
print(mymodel(5))
```

Output:

The example predicted the customer to spend 22.88 dollars, as seems to correspond to the diagram:

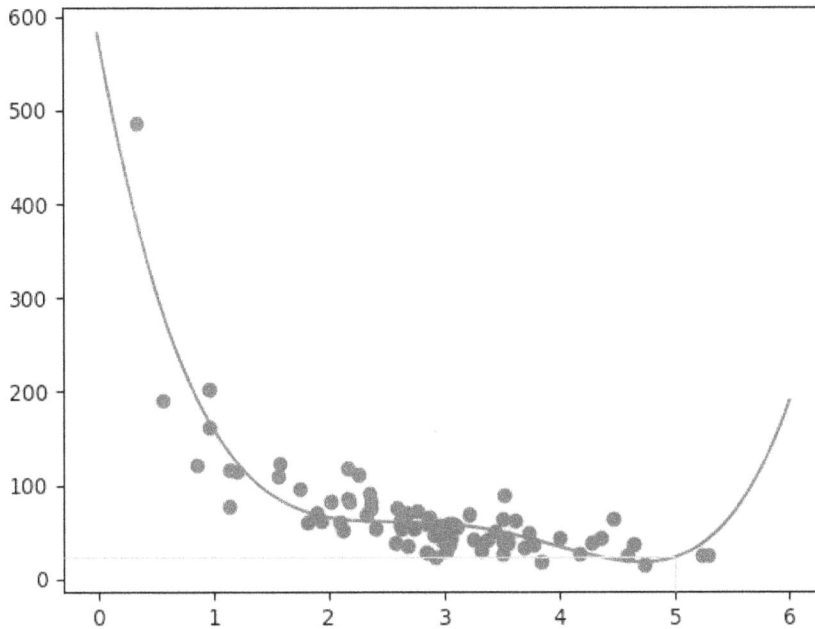

3.14 Decision Tree

The Decision Tree is a type of flow chart that may assist you in making choices based on past experience.

In an example, an individual is trying to determine whether or not to attend a comedy concert.

Fortunately, our example individual has registered each time a comedy event was scheduled in town, as well as some information on the comic and whether or not he or she attended.

Python can now design a decision tree based upon the data set to determine whether any new releases are worth seeing.

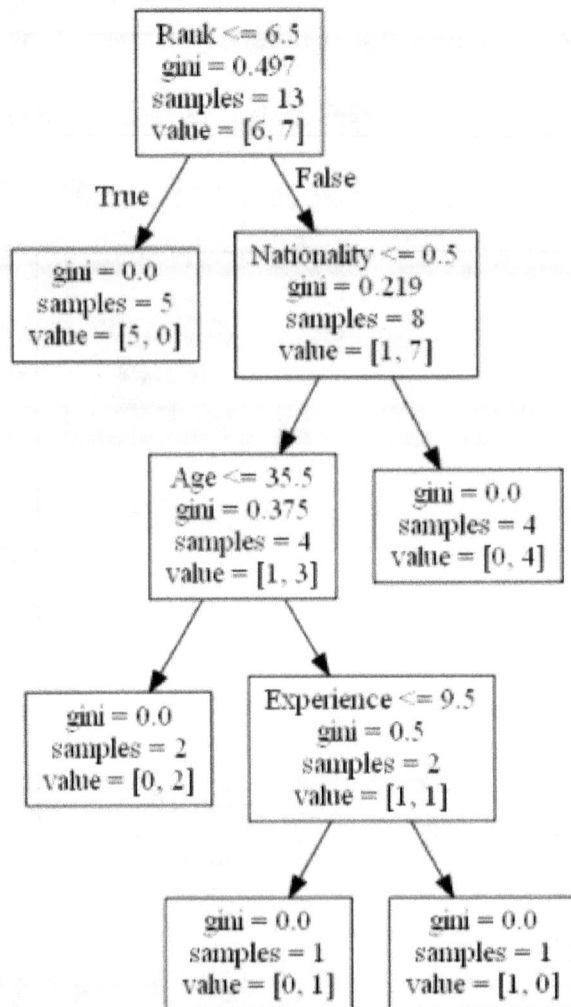

Working of decision tree:

First, load the modules you'll need, and then use pandas to read the dataset:

Example:

Read the data set and print it:

```
import pandas
from sklearn import tree
import pydotplus
from sklearn.tree import DecisionTreeClassifier
import matplotlib.pyplot as plt
import matplotlib.image as pltimg

df = pandas.read_csv("shows.csv")

print(df)
```

To create a decision tree, each of the information must be numerical.

The non-numerical columns 'Go' and 'Nationality' must be converted to numerical values.

The map() function in Pandas accepts a dictionary containing instructions on how to transform the values.

'UK': 0, 'USA': 1, 'N': 2' shows that convert 'UK' to 0, 'USA' to 1 then 'N' to 2.

Example:

Then we must segregate all feature columns from their target column by converting string values to numerical values.

```
d = {'UK': 0, 'USA': 1, 'N': 2}
df['Nationality'] = df['Nationality'].map(d)
d = {'YES': 1, 'NO': 0}
df['Go'] = df['Go'].map(d)

print(df)
```

These feature columns are just the ones we're trying to predict from, whereas the target column contains the values we're trying to forecast.

Example:

The feature columns are X, and the target column is y:

```
features = ['Age', 'Experience', 'Rank', 'Nationality']

X = df[features]
y = df['Go']

print(X)
print(y)
```

Now we can make the decision tree itself, fill it up with our information, and save it as an a.png file upon this computer:

Example:

Make the Decision Tree, saving it as a picture, and display it as follows:

```
dtree = DecisionTreeClassifier()
dtree = dtree.fit(X, y)
data = tree.export_graphviz(dtree, out_file=None, feature_names=features)
graph = pydotplus.graph_from_dot_data(data)
graph.write_png('mydecisiontree.png')

img=pltimg.imread('mydecisiontree.png')
imgplot = plt.imshow(img)
plt.show()
```

Python Feature Selection for Machine Learning

Feature selection is actually a method of selecting the characteristics in the data that give most to an output or prediction variable that you're interested in.

Many models, notably linear methods such as logistic or linear regression, suffer from the presence of irrelevant characteristics in their data.

The following are three advantages of completing selection of feature right before modeling your data:

Reduces Overfitting: When there is less duplicated data, there is less chance of making conclusions predicted on noise.

Modeling accuracy increases as a result of less/no deceptive data.

Lessens Training Time: With less data, algorithms may learn more quickly.

Machine Learning Feature Selection

Further section offers methods for feature selection techniques in Python.

Every recipe was created to be comprehensive and self-contained, allowing you to copy-and-paste it into your project and utilize it right away.

To explain the feature selection process, Recipes utilizes a Pima Indian diabetes dataset onset. It is the binary segmentation issue with just number attributes.

- Dataset Details.

- Dataset File.

1. Univariate Selection

Statistical tests may be performed to identify which attributes have the strongest link to an output variable.

The SelectKBest class in the scikit-learn package may be used with a variety of statistical tests to choose a certain range of attributes.

By this selection procedure, a variety of statistical tests may be applied. The ANOVA F-value approach, for example, is suited for categorical and numerical data, as shown in a Pima dataset. The f classif() method may be used to do this. In the example below, we'll use this strategy to choose the top four characteristics.

```
1  # Feature Selection with Univariate Statistical Tests
2  from pandas import read_csv
3  from numpy import set_printoptions
4  from sklearn.feature_selection import SelectKBest
5  from sklearn.feature_selection import f_classif
6  # load data
7  filename = 'pima-indians-diabetes.data.csv'
8  names = ['preg', 'plas', 'pres', 'skin', 'test', 'mass', 'pedi', 'age', 'class']
9  dataframe = read_csv(filename, names=names)
10 array = dataframe.values
11 X = array[:,0:8]
12 Y = array[:,8]
13 # feature extraction
14 test = SelectKBest(score_func=f_classif, k=4)
15 fit = test.fit(X, Y)
16 # summarize scores
17 set_printoptions(precision=3)
18 print(fit.scores_)
19 features = fit.transform(X)
20 # summarize selected features
21 print(features[0:5,:])
```

Because of the nonlinear dynamics of an algorithm or assessment technique, as well as changes in numerical accuracy, your findings may vary. Consider repeating the procedure and comparing the average result.

```
1  [ 39.67  213.162   3.257   4.304  13.281  71.772  23.871  46.141]
2
3  [[  6.  148.  33.6  50. ]
4   [  1.   85.  26.6  31. ]
5   [  8.  183.  23.3  32. ]
6   [  1.   89.  28.1  21. ]
7   [  0.  137.  43.1  33. ]]
```

You can see the scores for each attribute and the 4 attributes chosen.

2. Recursive Feature Elimination

Recursive Feature Elimination or RFE works by deleting characteristics iteratively and creating a model on the remaining attributes.

It determines which qualities (and combinations of characteristics) offer the most to determining the desired characteristic using model accuracy.

```
1  # Feature Extraction with RFE
2  from pandas import read_csv
3  from sklearn.feature_selection import RFE
4  from sklearn.linear_model import LogisticRegression
5  # load data
6  url = "https://raw.githubusercontent.com/jbrownlee/Datasets/master/pima-indians-di
7  names = ['preg', 'plas', 'pres', 'skin', 'test', 'mass', 'pedi', 'age', 'class']
8  dataframe = read_csv(url, names=names)
9  array = dataframe.values
10 X = array[:,0:8]
11 Y = array[:,8]
12 # feature extraction
13 model = LogisticRegression(solver='lbfgs')
14 rfe = RFE(model, 3)
15 fit = rfe.fit(X, Y)
16 print("Num Features: %d" % fit.n_features_)
17 print("Selected Features: %s" % fit.support_)
18 print("Feature Ranking: %s" % fit.ranking_)
```

To choose the top three characteristics, the example following uses RFE in conjunction with a logistic regression methodology. It doesn't matter whatever algorithm you choose as long as it's smart and consistent.

```
1  Num Features: 3
2  Selected Features: [ True False False False False  True  True False]
3  Feature Ranking: [1 2 3 5 6 1 1 4]
```

As you can see, RFE picked preg, mass, and pedi as the top three attributes.

These are denoted with the chosen one in the ranking_ array and True in a support array.

Principal Component Analysis

Principal Component Analysis or PCA compresses a dataset by applying linear algebra to it.

This is often referred to as a data reduction approach. PCA has the advantage of allowing you to select many dimensions and primary components in the converted outcome.

```
1  # Feature Extraction with PCA
2  import numpy
3  from pandas import read_csv
4  from sklearn.decomposition import PCA
5  # load data
6  url = "https://raw.githubusercontent.com/jbrownlee/Datasets/master/pima-indians-di
7  names = ['preg', 'plas', 'pres', 'skin', 'test', 'mass', 'pedi', 'age', 'class']
8  dataframe = read_csv(url, names=names)
9  array = dataframe.values
10 X = array[:,0:8]
11 Y = array[:,8]
12 # feature extraction
13 pca = PCA(n_components=3)
14 fit = pca.fit(X)
15 # summarize components
16 print("Explained Variance: %s" % fit.explained_variance_ratio_)
17 print(fit.components_)
```

We'll use PCA to determine three main components in the sample below.

```
1  Explained Variance: [ 0.88854663  0.06159078  0.02579012]
2  [[ -2.02176587e-03   9.78115765e-02   1.60930503e-02   6.07566861e-02
3      9.93110844e-01   1.40108085e-02   5.37167919e-04  -3.56474430e-03]
4   [  2.26488861e-02   9.72210040e-01   1.41909330e-01  -5.78614699e-02
5     -9.46266913e-02   4.69729766e-02   8.16804621e-04   1.40168181e-01]
6   [ -2.24649003e-02   1.43428710e-01  -9.22467192e-01  -3.07013055e-01
7      2.09773019e-02  -1.32444542e-01  -6.39983017e-04  -1.25454310e-01]]
```

The modified dataset (3 main components) has little similarity to the raw data, as can be shown.

Feature Importance

To evaluate the value of characteristics, bagged decision trees such as Extra Trees and Random Forest may be employed.

For such Pima Indian onset of diabetes dataset, we build an ExtraTreesClassifier classifier in the example below. The scikit-learn API has further information about the ExtraTreesClassifier class.

```
1  # Feature Importance with Extra Trees Classifier
2  from pandas import read_csv
3  from sklearn.ensemble import ExtraTreesClassifier
4  # load data
5  url = "https://raw.githubusercontent.com/jbrownlee/Datasets/master/pima-indians-d
6  names = ['preg', 'plas', 'pres', 'skin', 'test', 'mass', 'pedi', 'age', 'class']
7  dataframe = read_csv(url, names=names)
8  array = dataframe.values
9  X = array[:,0:8]
10 Y = array[:,8]
11 # feature extraction
12 model = ExtraTreesClassifier(n_estimators=10)
13 model.fit(X, Y)
14 print(model.feature_importances_)
```

As you can see, each attribute is assigned a significance score, with the higher the value, the more significant the attribute. The results point to the significance of plas, age, and mass.

```
1 [ 0.11070069  0.2213717   0.08824115  0.08068703  0.07281761  0.14548537 0.12654214
```

Chapter 4: Basic Syntax of the Python

Python has a lot of similarities with C, Perl, and Java. There are, nevertheless, some clear distinctions between the languages. A parser reads a Python program. Python was created to be a very readable programming language. The Python programming language's syntax is a collection of rules that dictate how a Python program is constructed.

4.1 Basic Python Program

Let's run several programs in various programming styles.

Interactive Mode Programming

When you use the interpreter without specifying a script file as an argument, you'll get the following message:

```
$ python
Python 2.4.3 (#1, Nov 11 2010, 13:34:43)
[GCC 4.1.2 20080704 (Red Hat 4.1.2-48)] on linux2
Type "help", "copyright", "credits" or "license" for more information.
>>>
```

At the Python prompt, write the following text and hit Enter.

```
>>> print "Hello, Python!"
```

If you're using a newer version of Python, you'll need to use the print statement with parentheses, as seen below. Hello, Python! In Python 2.4.3, however, this yields the following result.

```
Hello, Python!
```

Script Mode Programming

Invoking an interpreter with the script argument starts the script's execution and continues until it is completed. The interpreter is turned off after the script is done.

Let's develop a script for a basic Python app. The extension.py is used for Python files. In a test.py file, write the below source code:

```
print "Hello, Python!"
```

We'll presume you've placed the Python interpreter in your PATH variable. Now, try running this program like this:

```
$ python test.py
```

As a consequence of this, the following result is obtained:

```
Hello, Python!
```

Let's have a look at another technique to run a Python script. The amended test.py file may be found here:

```
#!/usr/bin/python

print "Hello, Python!"
```

We'll assume you have the Python interpreter in your /usr/bin directory. Now, try running this program like this:

```
$ chmod +x test.py     # This is to make file executable
$ ./test.py
```

As a consequence of this, the following result is obtained:

```
Hello, Python!
```

4.2 Python Identifiers

The Python identifier is really a name for a function, variable, class, module, or another object in Python. An identifier begins with a letter from A to Z, or a to z, or an underscore (_), then zero or even more letters, underscores, or numbers (0 to 9).

Within identifiers, punctuation characters like @, $, and percent are not allowed. Python is a programming language that is case-sensitive. As a result, in Python, manpower & Manpower are two separate identifiers.

The naming standards for Python identifiers are as follows:

- The name of the class begins using an uppercase letter. The beginning of all other identifiers is a lowercase letter.

- The presence of a single lead underscore in an identifier implies that it is private.

- An identification that begins with two lead underscores is considered to be very secret.

- An identifier is a language defined special name if it also terminates with two trailing underscores.

4.3 Reserved Words

The Python keywords are shown in the table below. You can't use these terms as constants, variables, and any similar identifier name since they're reserved. Only lowercase characters appear in the Python keywords.

and	exec	not
assert	finally	or
break	for	pass
class	from	print
continue	global	raise
def	if	return
del	import	try
elif	in	while
else	is	with
except	lambda	yield

4.4 Lines and Indentation

There are no brackets in Python to mark code blocks for function and class declarations or flow control. Line indentation, which is strictly enforced, is used to designate code blocks.

The indentation may be any number of spaces, but all statements as in block should be indented the same amount. For instance:

```
if True:
    print "True"
else:
    print "False"
```

The next block, however, produces an error:

```
if True:
print "Answer"
print "True"
else:
print "Answer"
print "False"
```

Thus, in Python, a block is formed by all continuous lines indented by the same amount of spaces. Various statement blocks are used in the following example:

```python
#!/usr/bin/python

import sys

try:
    # open file stream
    file = open(file_name, "w")
except IOError:
    print "There was an error writing to", file_name
    sys.exit()
print "Enter '", file_finish,
print "' When finished"
while file_text != file_finish:
    file_text = raw_input("Enter text: ")
    if file_text == file_finish:
        # close the file
        file.close
        break
    file.write(file_text)
    file.write("\n")
file.close()
file_name = raw_input("Enter filename: ")
if len(file_name) == 0:
    print "Next time please enter something"
    sys.exit()
try:
    file = open(file_name, "r")
except IOError:
    print "There was an error reading file"
    sys.exit()
file_text = file.read()
file.close()
print file_text
```

4.5 Multi-Line Statements

In Python, statements usually conclude on a new line. A line continuation character () in Python, on the other hand, may be used to indicate that a line should continue. Such as:

```python
total = item_one + \
        item_two + \
        item_three
```

A line continuation character is not required for statements enclosed in the [],() or {}. For example in the case:

```
days = ['Monday', 'Tuesday', 'Wednesday',
         'Thursday', 'Friday']
```

4.6 Quotation in Python

To designate string literals, Python allows single ('), double ("), and triple ("' or """) quotes, as long as the same kind of quotation begins and ends the string.

To spread the string over many lines, triple quotes are utilized. All of the following, for example, is lawful:

```
word = 'word'
sentence = "This is a sentence."
paragraph = """This is a paragraph. It is
made up of multiple lines and sentences."""
```

4.7 Comments in Python

A comment starts with a hash mark (#) outside of a string literal. A Python interpreter ignores any characters following the # and up till the end of a physical line as part of the remark.

```
#!/usr/bin/python

# First comment
print "Hello, Python!" # second comment
```

As a consequence of this, the following result is obtained:

```
Hello, Python!
```

Following a statement or expression, you may write a remark on the same line:

```
name = "Madisetti" # This is again comment
```

You may remark on many lines in the same way:

```
# This is a comment.
# This is a comment, too.
# This is a comment, too.
# I said that already.
```

The Python interpreter ignores the following triple-quoted text, which may be applied as a multiline comment:

```
'''
This is a multiline
comment.
'''
```

Using Blank Lines

A blank line is a line that has simply whitespace, potentially with a comment, and Python ignores it completely.

To end a multiline statement during an interactive interpreter process, type an empty physical line.

Waiting for the User

The program's next line shows the prompt and the phrase "Press your enter key to leave," and then waits for a user to respond:

Before showing the real line, "\n\n" is used to produce two additional lines. The application finishes when the user pushes the key. This is a clever way to keep a terminal window active until the user has completed their task.

Multiple Statements on a Single Line

If neither statement begins a new code block, a semicolon (;) permits several statements on a single line. Here's an example of how to use the semicolon:

```
import sys; x = 'foo'; sys.stdout.write(x + '\n')
```

Multiple Statement Groups as Suites

In Python, a suite is a collection of discrete statements that form a single code block. The header line or a suite are required for compound or complicated statements like while, if, def, and class.

The statement containing the keyword is started with a header line, which ends with a colon (:), and is continued by one or multiple lines that build up the suite.

For instance:

```
if expression :
    suite
elif expression :
    suite
else :
    suite
```

Command Line Arguments

Many applications may be launched to offer you basic instructions on how to use them. This is possible using Python's -h – helper function.

```
$ python -h
usage: python [option] ... [-c cmd | -m mod | file | -] [arg] ...
Options and arguments (and corresponding environment variables):
-c cmd : program passed in as string (terminates option list)
-d     : debug output from parser (also PYTHONDEBUG=x)
-E     : ignore environment variables (such as PYTHONPATH)
-h     : print this help message and exit

[ etc. ]
```

You may also program your script such that it accepts a variety of parameters.

4.8 Python Coding Style

There should be four spaces between each indentation with no tabs.

Do not use tabs and spaces in the same sentence. Tabs cause confusion, therefore it's best to stick to using just spaces.

Users with a tiny display will appreciate the maximum line length of 79 characters.

Split class and top-level function declarations with blank lines, and use a solitary blank line to differentiate methods declarations within a class and bigger chunks of code within functions.

Inline comments should be used whenever feasible should be complete sentences.

Around expressions and assertions, use spaces.

Python Reserve words:

The identifiers listed below are reserved terms in the language that can be used as regular identifiers.

False	class	finally	is	return
None	continue	for	lambda	try
True	def	from	nonlocal	while
and	del	global	not	with
as	el	if	or	yield
assert	else	import	pass	
break	except	in	raise	

Chapter 5: Statements in python

A Python Statement

Statements are the instructions that a Python interpreter may carry out. An assignment statement, for example, is a = 1. Other types of statements include if statements, for statements, while statements, and so on, which will be addressed later.

Multi-line statement

A newline character is used to indicate the conclusion of a statement in Python. However, using the line continuation character, we may have a statement span many lines (\). Consider the following scenario:

```
a = 1 + 2 + 3 + \
    4 + 5 + 6 + \
    7 + 8 + 9
```

This is a line continuation that is explicitly stated. Brackets [ ], Parentheses ( ), and braces { } in Python imply line continuation. For example, we may write the multi-line sentence as follows:

```
a = (1 + 2 + 3 +
    4 + 5 + 6 +
    7 + 8 + 9)
```

The line continuation is implied by the enclosing parenthesis ( ). The same is true for [ ] and. Consider the following scenario:

```
colors = ['red',
          'blue',
          'green']
```

We may also use semicolons to place numerous statements on a single line, as seen below:

```
a = 1; b = 2; c = 3
```

Chapter 6: Dictionaries in python

The dictionary in python is actually a list of elements that are not in any particular order. A dictionary contains a key/value pair for each entry.

When the key is known, dictionaries are optimized to retrieve values.

6.1 Creating Python Dictionary

It's as easy as putting things within curly braces and separating them with commas to make a dictionary.

The one item has one key and its value, which are stated as a pair key as a value.

Although values may be of either any data type and may be repeated, keys necessarily be unique and of an immutable type i.e. integer, string or tuple along immutable members.

```python
# empty dictionary
my_dict = {}

# dictionary with integer keys
my_dict = {1: 'apple', 2: 'ball'}

# dictionary with mixed keys
my_dict = {'name': 'John', 1: [2, 4, 3]}

# using dict()
my_dict = dict({1:'apple', 2:'ball'})

# from sequence having each item as a pair
my_dict = dict([(1,'apple'), (2,'ball')])
```

So you can observe from the above example, in addition we can use the built-in dict() method to construct a dictionary.

6.2 Accessing Elements from Dictionary

While other data types utilize indexing to obtain values, a dictionary employs keys. Keys may be utilized using the get() function or within square brackets [].

When we use square brackets [], we get a KeyError if a key isn't located in the dictionary. The get() function, but on the other hand, yields None if a key isn't found.

```python
# get vs [] for retrieving elements
my_dict = {'name': 'Jack', 'age': 26}

# Output: Jack
print(my_dict['name'])

# Output: 26
print(my_dict.get('age'))

# Trying to access keys which doesn't exist throws error
# Output None
print(my_dict.get('address'))

# KeyError
print(my_dict['address'])
```

Output:

```
Jack
26
None
Traceback (most recent call last):
  File "<string>", line 15, in <module>
    print(my_dict['address'])
KeyError: 'address'
```

6.3 Changing and Adding Dictionary elements

Dictionaries are subject to change. Using the assignment operator, we may create latest items or alter the value of already presented ones.

If the key already exists, the existing value will be changed. If the key is missing, the dictionary is updated with a new key as a value pair.

```python
# Changing and adding Dictionary Elements
my_dict = {'name': 'Jack', 'age': 26}

# update value
my_dict['age'] = 27

#Output: {'age': 27, 'name': 'Jack'}
print(my_dict)

# add item
my_dict['address'] = 'Downtown'

# Output: {'address': 'Downtown', 'age': 27, 'name': 'Jack'}
print(my_dict)
```

Output:

```
{'name': 'Jack', 'age': 27}
{'name': 'Jack', 'age': 27, 'address': 'Downtown'}
```

6.4 Removing elements from Dictionary

Using the pop() function, we may delete a specific item from a dictionary. This function returns the value after removing an item with a supplied key. The popitem() function removes and returns any key, value item pair from a dictionary. The clear() function may be used to delete all of the objects at once.

A keyword del may also be used to delete specific entries or the whole vocabulary.

```python
# create a dictionary
squares = {1: 1, 2: 4, 3: 9, 4: 16, 5: 25}

# remove a particular item, returns its value
# Output: 16
print(squares.pop(4))

# Output: {1: 1, 2: 4, 3: 9, 5: 25}
print(squares)

# remove an arbitrary item, return (key,value)
# Output: (5, 25)
print(squares.popitem())

# Output: {1: 1, 2: 4, 3: 9}
print(squares)

# remove all items
squares.clear()

# Output: {}
print(squares)

# delete the dictionary itself
del squares

# Throws Error
print(squares)
```

Output:

```
16
{1: 1, 2: 4, 3: 9, 5: 25}
(5, 25)
{1: 1, 2: 4, 3: 9}
{}
Traceback (most recent call last):
  File "<string>", line 30, in <module>
    print(squares)
NameError: name 'squares' is not defined
```

6.5 Methods for Python Dictionary

The methods that may be used with the dictionary are listed underneath. While few of these have previously been mentioned in the previous paragraphs.

Method	Description
clear()	Removes all items from the dictionary.
copy()	Returns a shallow copy of the dictionary.
fromkeys(seq[, v])	Returns a new dictionary with keys from `seq` and value equal to `v` (defaults to `None`).
get(key[,d])	Returns the value of the `key`. If the `key` does not exist, returns `d` (defaults to `None`).
items()	Return a new object of the dictionary's items in (key, value) format.
keys()	Returns a new object of the dictionary's keys.
pop(key[,d])	Removes the item with the `key` and returns its value or `d` if `key` is not found. If `d` is not provided and the `key` is not found, it raises `KeyError`.
popitem()	Removes and returns an arbitrary item (**key, value**). Raises `KeyError` if the dictionary is empty.
setdefault(key[,d])	Returns the corresponding value if the `key` is in the dictionary. If not, inserts the `key` with a value of `d` and returns `d` (defaults to `None`).
update([other])	Updates the dictionary with the key/value pairs from `other`, overwriting existing keys.
values()	Returns a new object of the dictionary's values

Following are a few examples of how these strategies may be used.

```
# Dictionary Methods
marks = {}.fromkeys(['Math', 'English', 'Science'], 0)

# Output: {'English': 0, 'Math': 0, 'Science': 0}
print(marks)

for item in marks.items():
    print(item)

# Output: ['English', 'Math', 'Science']
print(list(sorted(marks.keys())))
```

Output:

```
# Dictionary Methods
marks = {}.fromkeys(['Math', 'English', 'Science'], 0)

# Output: {'English': 0, 'Math': 0, 'Science': 0}
print(marks)

for item in marks.items():
    print(item)

# Output: ['English', 'Math', 'Science']
print(list(sorted(marks.keys())))
```

6.6 Python Dictionary Comprehension

In Python, dictionary comprehension is actually a simple and beautiful approach to generate a new dictionary via an iterable.

An expression pair key is a value follows by a for statement enclosed in curly braces in dictionary comprehension.

Here's an example of a dictionary for each entry consisting of a pair of numbers and their squares.

234

```
# Dictionary Comprehension
squares = {x: x*x for x in range(6)}

print(squares)
```

Output:

```
{0: 0, 1: 1, 2: 4, 3: 9, 4: 16, 5: 25}
```

This code is the same as

```
squares = {}
for x in range(6):
    squares[x] = x*x
print(squares)
```

Output:

```
{0: 0, 1: 1, 2: 4, 3: 9, 4: 16, 5: 25}
```

More for or if statements may be included in a dictionary comprehension if desired.

Items may be filtered out using the optional if statement to create a new dictionary.

Here are several examples of how to construct an odd-item dictionary.

```
# Dictionary Comprehension with if conditional
odd_squares = {x: x*x for x in range(11) if x % 2 == 1}

print(odd_squares)
```

Output:

```
{1: 1, 3: 9, 5: 25, 7: 49, 9: 81}
```

6.7 Other Dictionary Operations

Dictionary Membership Test

Using the term in, we can see whether the key will be in a dictionary or not. It's worth noting that a membership test only applies to the keys, not the values.

```python
# Membership Test for Dictionary Keys
squares = {1: 1, 3: 9, 5: 25, 7: 49, 9: 81}

# Output: True
print(1 in squares)

# Output: True
print(2 not in squares)

# membership tests for key only not value
# Output: False
print(49 in squares)
```

Output:

```
True
True
False
```

Using a Dictionary to Iterate

A for loop may be used to cycle across every key in the dictionary.

```
# Iterating through a Dictionary
squares = {1: 1, 3: 9, 5: 25, 7: 49, 9: 81}
for i in squares:
    print(squares[i])
```

Output:

```
1
9
25
49
81
```

Dictionary's Built-in Functions

All(), len(), cmp(), any(), sorted(), and other built-in methods are widely used along dictionaries to complete various tasks.

Function	Description
all()	Return `True` if all keys of the dictionary are True (or if the dictionary is empty).
any()	Return `True` if any key of the dictionary is true. If the dictionary is empty, return `False`.
len()	Return the length (the number of items) in the dictionary.
cmp()	Compares items of two dictionaries. (Not available in Python 3)
sorted()	Return a new sorted list of keys in the dictionary.

Below are some examples of how to operate with a dictionary using built-in functions.

```
# Dictionary Built-in Functions
squares = {0: 0, 1: 1, 3: 9, 5: 25, 7: 49, 9: 81}

# Output: False
print(all(squares))

# Output: True
print(any(squares))

# Output: 6
print(len(squares))

# Output: [0, 1, 3, 5, 7, 9]
print(sorted(squares))
```

Output:

```
False
True
6
[0, 1, 3, 5, 7, 9]
```

Chapter 7: First Project Of Python

Implementing the First Program

Step: 1

 Launch PyCharm Editor. The PyCharm introduction screen may be seen here.
Click "Create New Project" to start a new project.

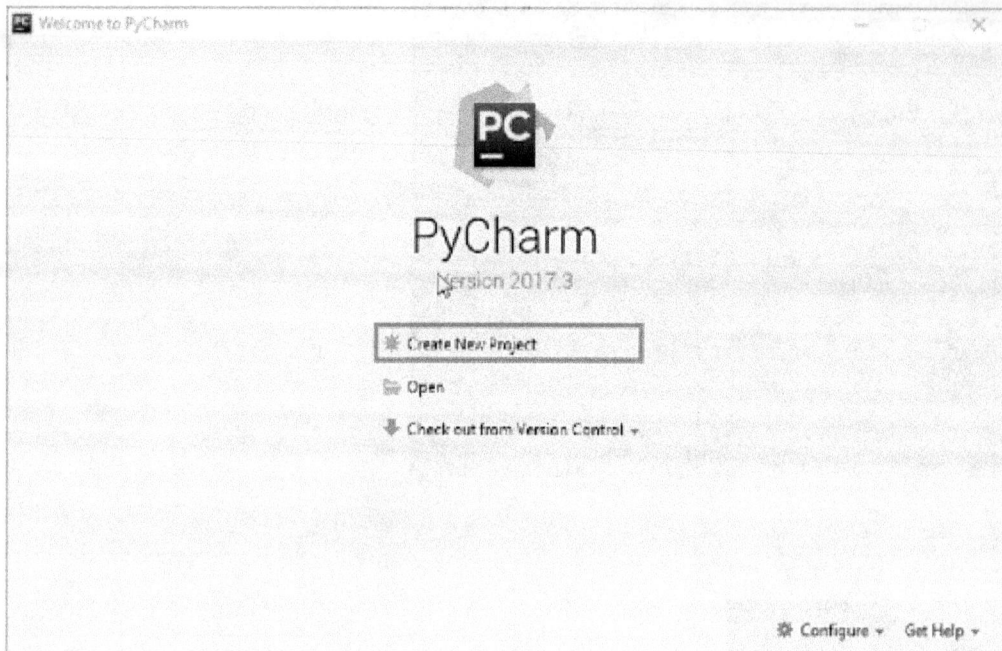

Step: 2

You'll have to choose a place.

You have the option of choosing the place where the project will be developed. Keep it as is if you don't want to alter the location, but change the title from "untitled" to something more significant, such as "FirstProject."

PyCharm should have discovered any Python interpreter you previously installed.

Then press the "Create" button.

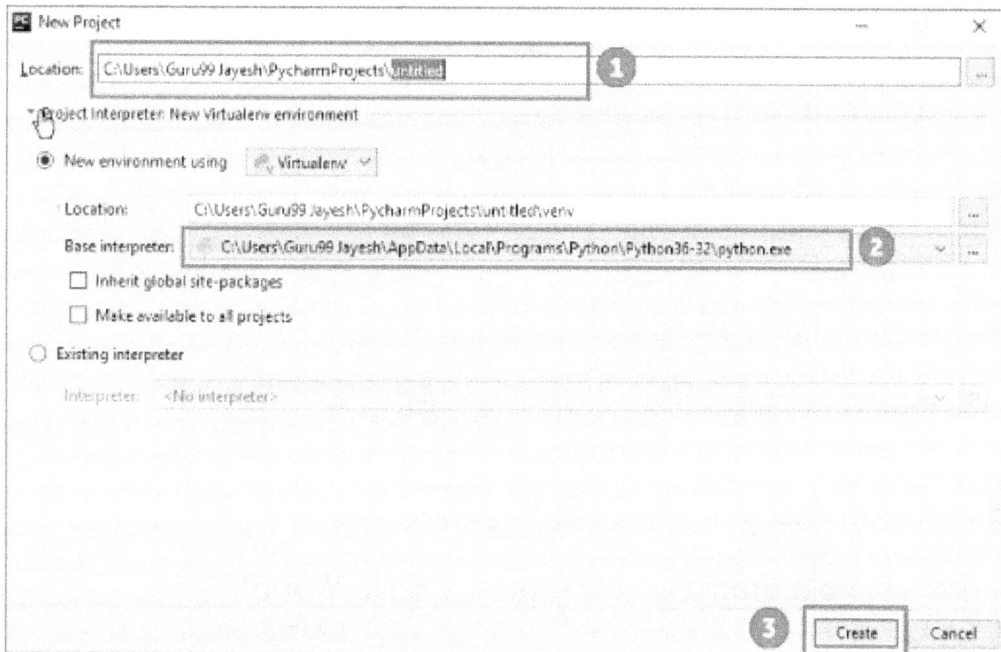

Step: 3

Now it's your turn. Go to the "File" menu and choose "New." After that, choose "Python File."

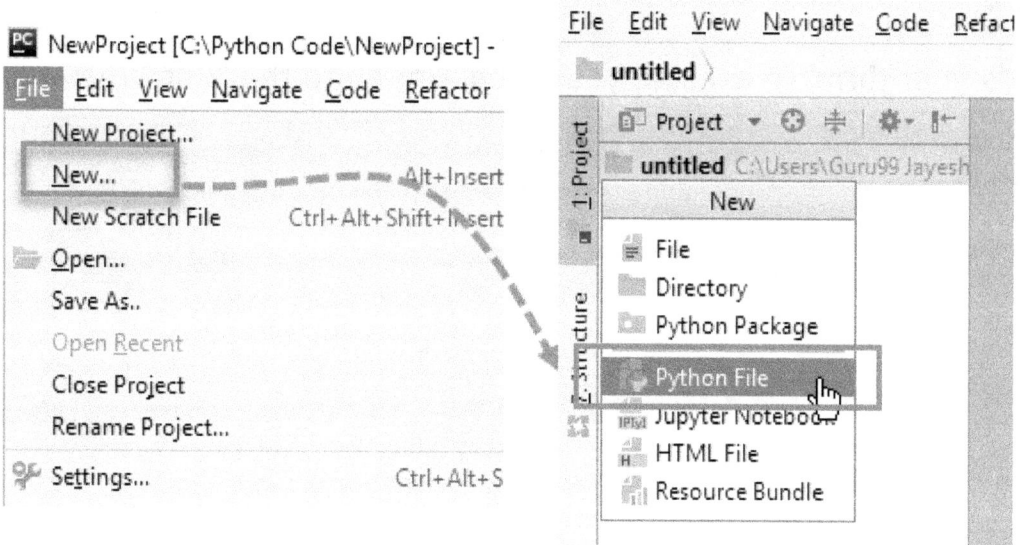

Step: 4

A new pop-up window will open. Now input the file's name (in this case, "HelloWorld") and click "OK."

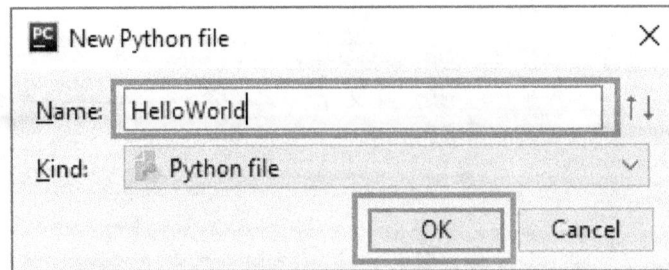

Step: 5

Now create a simple program called print ('Hello World!').

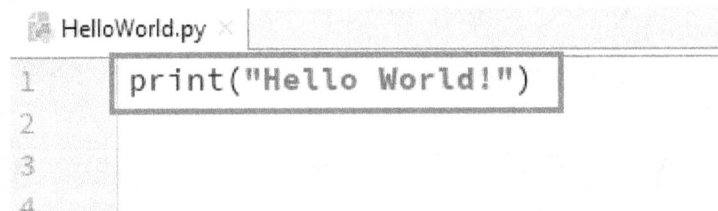

Step: 6

Now it's your turn. To execute your program, go to the "Run" menu and pick "Run."

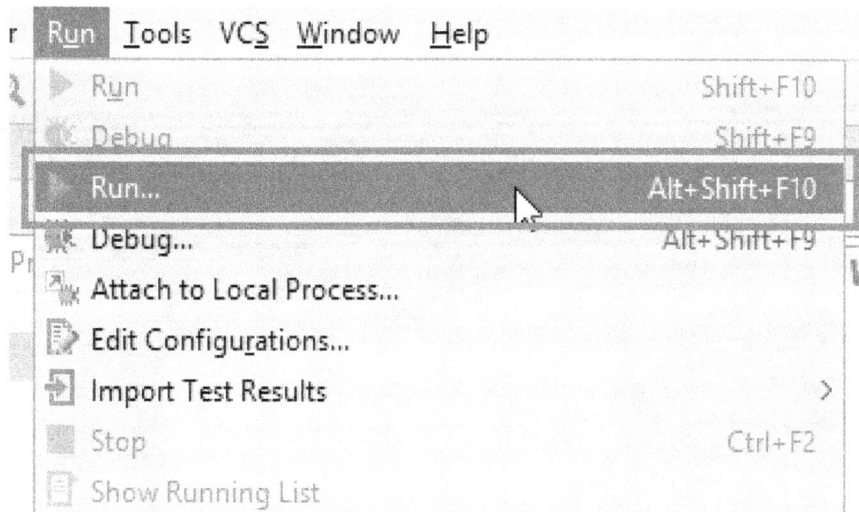

Step: 7

The result of your application may be shown at a bottom of the screen.

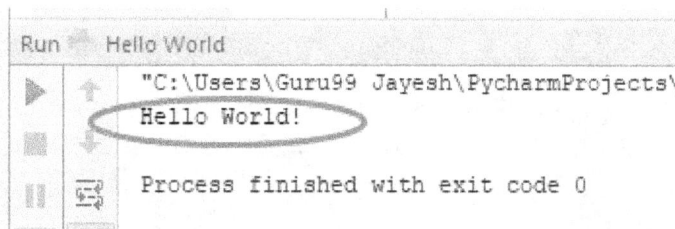

Step: 8

You may still execute a code from a command prompt if you're not using Pycharm Editor installed. To execute the software, type the right file location at the command prompt.

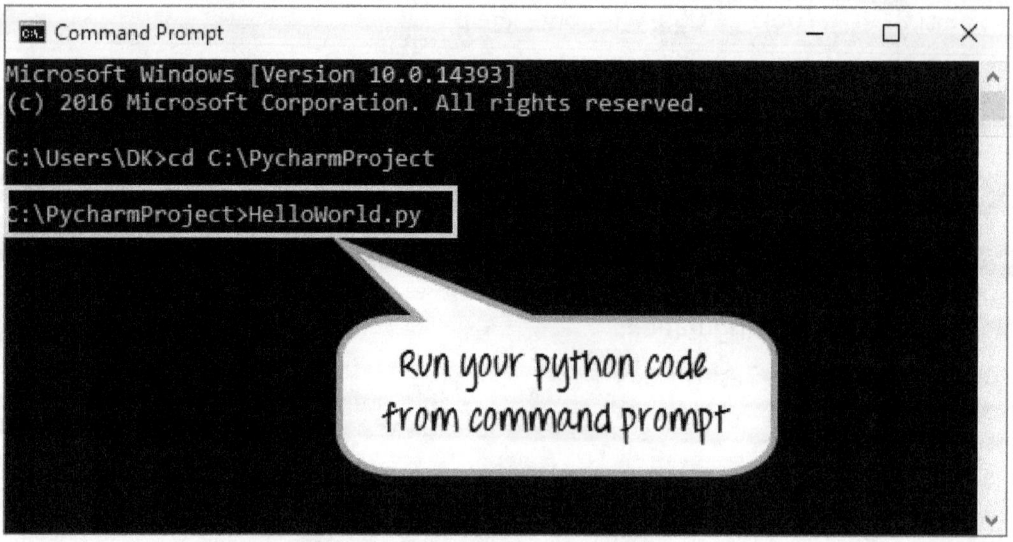

The code's output would be as follows:

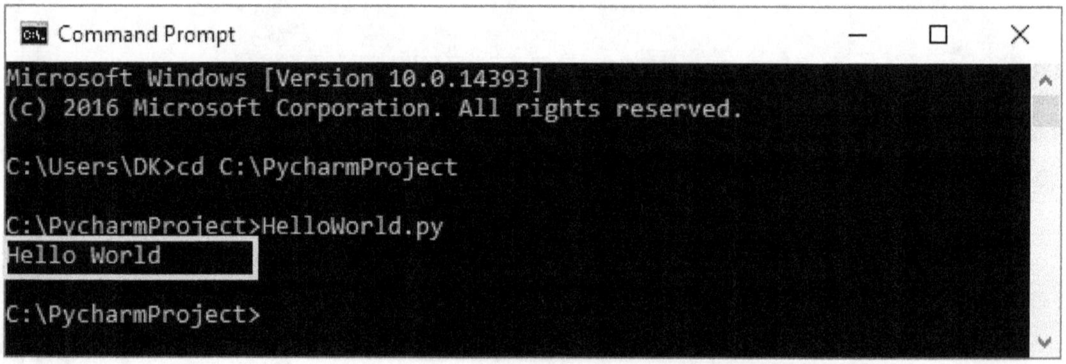

Chapter 8: Indexes In python

In Python, what is indexing?

In Python, indexing is a method of referring to particular elements inside an iterable based on their location. In other words, you may directly access your desired pieces inside an iterable and perform a variety of actions based on your requirements.

Before we go into Python indexing examples, there's something to keep in mind:

Objects in Python are "zero-indexed," which means the position count begins at zero. A similar pattern may be seen in many different programming languages. Because of its online popularity in meme culture, several of you should already be acquainted with it.

So, let's say there are five items on a list. The "zeroth" position is then held by an element i.e. the leftmost element, followed by the elements in a first, second, third, and fourth place.

```python
fruits = ["apple", "grape", "orange", "guava", "banana"]

#Printing out the indexes of Apples and Banana
print("Indedx of Apple: " + fruits.index("apple"))
print("Indedx of Banana: " + fruits.index("banana"))
```

Output:

```
Indedx of Apple: 0
Indedx of Banana: 4
```

Once an index() method is invoked on a list with an item name as a parameter, the index of a particular item inside the list may be exposed.

Finally, we'll look at how to utilize the index() function on iterable objects in the next section.

8.1 What is the Index Operator in Python?

A Python Index Operator is symbolized by square brackets that open and close: []. The syntax, on the other hand, necessitates the use of a number within the brackets.

Syntax of Python Index Operator:

```
ObjectName[n] #Where n is just an integer number that represents the position
```

8.2 Indexing in Python: A Step-by-Step Guide

We'll look at several instances of indexing in Python in the sections below.

1. Indexing Strings Output:

```
greetings = "Hello, World!"

print(greetings[0]) #Prints the 0-th element in our string

print(greetings[5]) #Prints the 5-th element in our string

print(greetins[12]) #Prints the 12-th element in our string
```

We can observe how our print method accesses several components inside our given string object to obtain the desired characters.

H
,
!

2. Negative Indexing in Python

We just learned how to utilize indexing in Strings and Lists to retrieve the precise objects we're looking for. Although we've used a positive integer within our index operator the square brackets in all of our prior examples, this isn't required.

Negative integers are often used if we are concerned about the final few members of a list or simply wish to index a list from the other end. Negative indexing is the technique of indexing from an opposite end.

```python
letters = ['a', 's', 'd', 'f']

#We want to print the last element of the list
print(letters[-1]) #Notice we didn't use -0

#To print the 2nd last element from an iterable
print(letters[-2])
```

The final element in negative indexing is denoted by -1 rather than -0.

Output:

f
d

Chapter 9: Installation of python

Python Installation Instructions; Set-up for Environment:

The first step toward becoming a Python developer is to understand how to install and update Python on any local system or computer. We'll go through how to install Python on different operating systems in this article.

9.1 Installation on Windows:

To get the newest version of Python, go to https://www.python.org/downloads/. We will install Python 3.8.6 on the Windows operating system through this procedure. When we click the link above, we will be sent to the following website.

1st step:

 Choose the Python version you want to download.

Select the "Download" option from the drop-down menu.

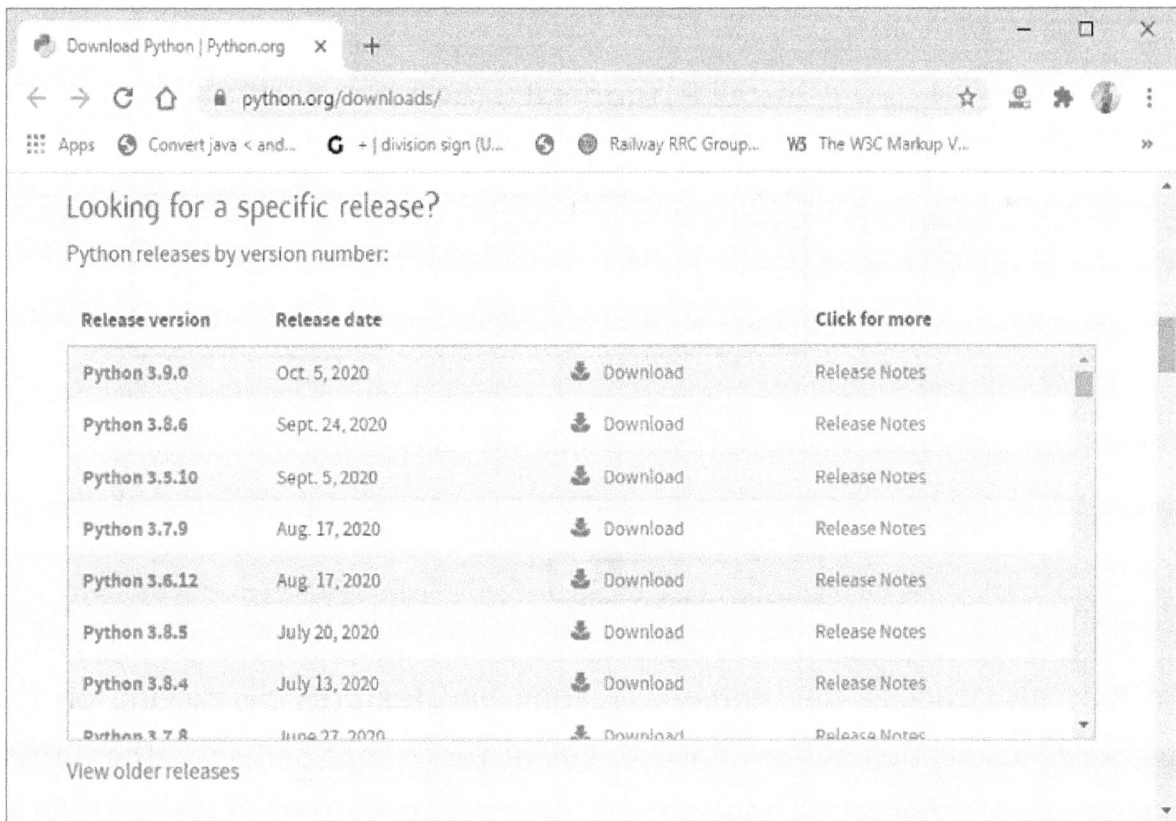

Step 2:

Select the Install Now option.

Double-click the downloaded executable file to bring up the following window. Proceed by selecting Customize installation. When you choose to Add a Path check box, the Python path will be automatically configured.

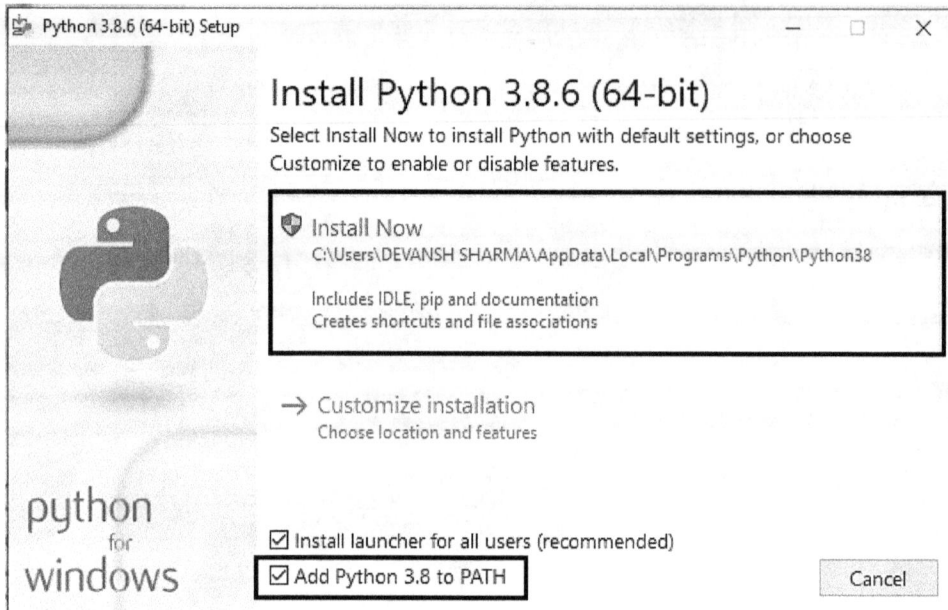

We may also choose the required location and features by clicking on the customize installation button. Another key factor to consider is whether or not to install a launcher for all users.

Step 3:

In-Process Installation

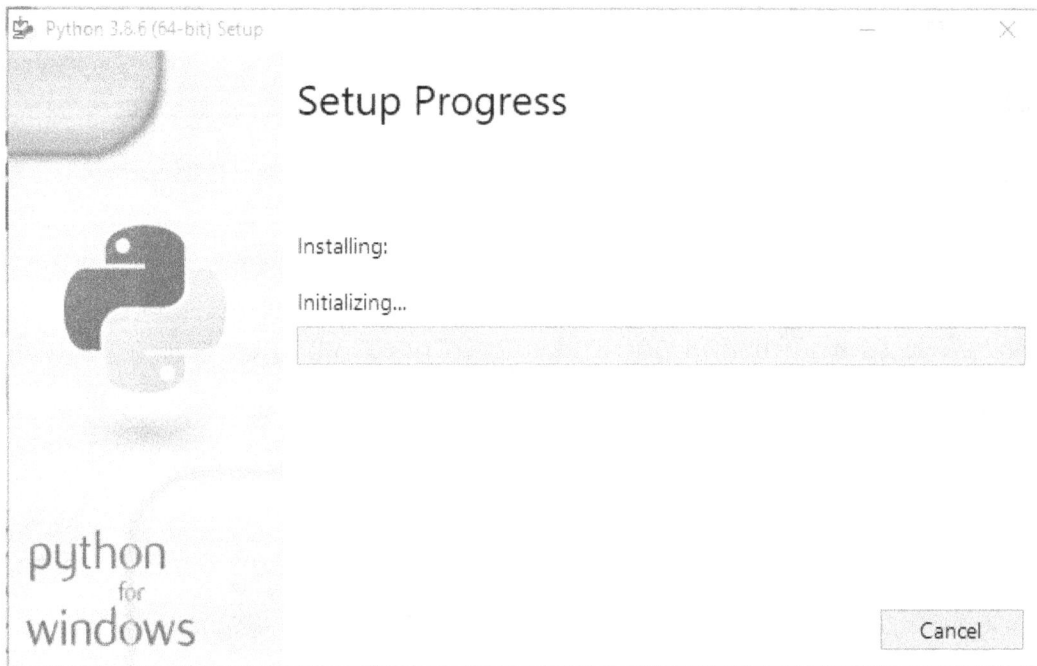

Try running python from the command prompt now. If you're using Python 3, use the python -version.

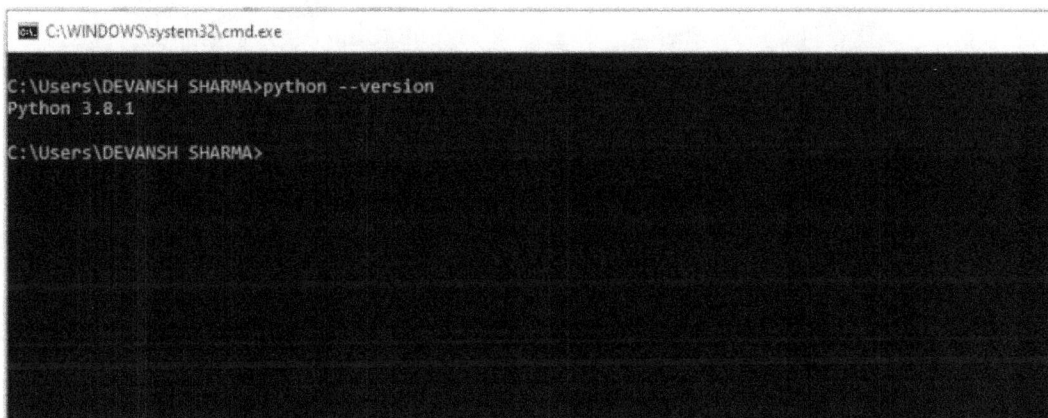

We're all set to work with Python.

Basic hints and tips to help you become a smart developer

Following are the helpful tricks for newbies:

1) Swapping numbers:

When it refers to algorithms and data structures, swapping is a crucial topic. Let's look at how to swap numbers in Python.

The Conventional Approach:

Here, we'll have to make a temporary variable to store values so that the other one can become empty and the values can be swapped.

```
x=5
y=10
temp=x
x=y
y=temp
print("The value of x after swapping is",x)
print("The value of y after swapping is",y)
```

Now, I'll show you a quick way to swap figures in Python.

```
x = 5
y = 10
x, y = y, x
print("The value of x after swapping is",x)
print("The value of y after swapping is",y)
```

2) Reversing a String

Reversing a string can't get much easier than this, so be careful. We'll utilize a basic negative indexing and string slicing approach. We see that Python may have negative indexes, so we slice it and don't provide a beginning or ending value; instead, we provide a range of -1, which means it will reverse the indexes from the last to the first.

```python
word = "orehgnimmargorp"
print(word[: : -1])
```

Result:

programming hero

Simple slicing is sufficient to complete the task.

3) String Concatenation

It is among the most valuable and practical tips. Let's look at how to make a string out of a set of characters The join() function will be used. Let's have a glance at how it works.

```python
characters = ['p', 'y', 't', 'h', 'o', 'n']
word = "".join(characters)
print(word)
```

Result:

Python

4) Using ZIP with lists

To merge numerous lists with the equal length and output the result, use the zip() method.

```
language = ["python", "java", "c"]
creators = ["guido van rossum", "james gosling", "denis ricthie"]
for language, creators in zip(language, creators):
    print(language, creators)
```

Result:

```
python guido van rossum
java james gosling
c denis ricthie
```

5) The _ Operator

It's possible that you've never heard of the operator before. An output of the last performed expression is represented by. Let's have a look at how it works.

```
>>> 2+ 3
5
>>> _       # the _ operator, it will return the output of the last executed statement.
>>> 5
```

6) Creating a dictionary from a list

When working on actual Machine learning and Django projects, this is one of the most effective strategies. As previously, use the zip() method, but this time use it from the dictionary function Object().

```
user = ["Peter", "John", "Sam"]
age = [23,19,34]
dictionary = dict(zip(user, age))
print(dictionary)
```

Result:

```
{"Peter" : 23, "John" : 23, "Sam" : 34}
```

7) Opening a website

Python is really about having fun. One of the greatest methods is to use a python script to access a webpage.

```
import webbrowser
webbrowser.open("https://www.programming-hero.com/")
```

This is how a website may be launched using only one line of code.

8) Multiple users input

If you're thinking, 'It's easy, simply utilize two input functions, and we're done," you're correct. But I have a better way of accomplishing it; first, let's look at the old school method.

```
x = input("Enter a number")
y = input ("Enter another number")
print(x)
print(y)
```

The more pleasant option,

```
x, y = input("Enter a two values: ").split()
print("value of x ", x)
print("value of y: ", y)
```

The split() method allows you to obtain several inputs from a user. The supplied separator is used to divide up the provided input. If no separator is specified, any white space serves as a separator.

9) The Walrus:= Operator

One of Python's most recent features is the Walrus operator. Python 3.8 was the first version to include it. It's an expression of assignment that enables you to assign values to the expression directly.

The Conventional Approach:

```python
xs = [1,2,3]
n=len(xs)
if n>2:
    print(n)
```

In the following example, first, define a list and afterward assign the length of a list to a variable called n.

With the help of walrus operators,

```python
xs = [1,2,3]
if (n:=len(xs)>2):
    print(n)
```

We declare and assign a value at the same time in this case. That is the Walrus operator's power.

10) Colored Text

Are you tired of your old white and black console? This ruse is meant to save you.

```python
from termcolor import colored
print(colored("Programming Hero", "yellow"))
print(colored("Programming Hero", "red"))
```

Result:

```
Programming Hero
Programming Hero
```

11) List comprehension

In Python, list comprehension provides a beautiful approach to define and generate lists. We can make lists in the same way as we can make mathematical assertions, but only on one line. The syntax for list comprehension is more straightforward. It's a clever approach to working with lists...

The Conventional Approach:

The code below provides a series of odd square values.

```python
odd_square = []
for x in range(1, 11):
    if x % 2 == 1:
        odd_square.append(x**2)
print (odd_square)
```

How to Use List Comprehension:

In the same line, we may have an expression, a loop, and a condition. In only one line, you may write 5 lines of code. That's how you understand a list.

```
odd_square = [x ** 2 for x in range(1, 11) if x % 2 == 1]
(print odd_square)
```

12) Shutting down a computer

Let's look at how to shut down a computer with only one single line of code. We will utilize the OS module for this. It's one of Python's most significant modules, with a slew of additional features.

```
import os
os.system('shutdown -s')
```

13) Multi-args Function:

It's one of Python's coolest tricks. Let's imagine you're writing the function and you don't know how many parameters the user will provide. So, how do we define the function's parameters? Multi-args functions are used to add any amount of values given by the user. See the example below.

```
def add(*num):
    result=0
    for i in num:
        result=result+i
    return result

print(add(1,2))
print(add(1,2,3,4,5))
```

Result:

```
                    3
                    15
```

As a result, the multi-args function constructs a list of arguments before carrying out the action.

14) Palindrome

I'm sure you've run across this issue before. This is definitely one of the institution's most popular issues. Have you ever considered doing anything using only one line of code?

```
word = "wow"
palindrome = bool(word.find(word[: : -1]) + 1)
print(palindrome)
```

Result:

```
                    True
```

15) Passwords are read as user input.

Provide a positive user experience even with basic menu-based apps. To read passwords from users in terminal apps, use the getpass module.

```
            username : john23
            password : *******
```

Result:

```
from getpass import getpass

username = input('username : ')
password = getpass('password : ' )
```

This conceals a user input for a console's password field.

16) Fibonacci series

Oh, that's a famous coding issue at another institution. I've got another easy one-line answer for you. Amaze your instructor by throwing this code at him or her.

```
fibo = lambda n : n if n <= 1 else fibo(n-1) + fibo(n-2)
result = fibo(10)
print(result)
```

17) Measuring the Time It Takes to Execute a Task

Do you want to put your software to the test? Do you want to keep track of your performance and execution time? This function will be quite beneficial. Let's try it out.

```
import time
startTime = time.time()

# your code

endTime = time.time()
totalTime = endTime - startTime
print("Execute code is= ", totalTime)
```

The milliseconds it takes for the program to run will be output, which will aid in improving performance and modifying the code appropriately.

18) Lambda Function

Because these functions don't have names, they're also known as anonymous functions. These are commonly used for Data Science, Machine Learning, Django backends, and other fields. Let's have a look at an example of how to add two integers.

Typical Function:

```
def add(a,b):
    return a + b

add(2,3)
```

Lambda Function:

```
add = lambda a,b : a+b
add(2,3)
```

19) Tuple Manipulation

What exactly is it? How are we going to do it? How can we alter tuples if we know they're immutable? Yes, we can! Because we are programmers, we can solve any difficulty. Consider the case below.

```
tuple1=(1,2,3,4,5)
list1=list(tuple1)
list1.append(6)
tuple2=tuple(list1)
print(tuple2)
```

Result:

```
(1,2,3,4,5,6)
```

Is it really that simple? It's as simple as using the list() and tuple() constructors.

20) Getting rid of duplicates in a List:

Duplicate items are possible in lists. However, there are times when duplicate entries in the list are undesirable. Let's have a look at how it can be accomplished.

```
listNumbers = [20, 22, 24, 26, 28, 28, 20, 30, 24]
print("Original= ", listNumbers)
listNumbers = list(set(listNumbers))
print("After removing duplicate= ", listNumbers)
```

Result:

```
Original = [20, 22, 24, 26, 28, 28, 20, 30, 24]
After removing duplicate = [20, 22, 24, 26, 28, 30]
```

I hope these tips will help you improve your Python skills, and it was a lot of fun!

Conclusion:

Python is a high-level programming language that is dynamically semantic, interpreted, and object-oriented. Its built-in high-level data structures make it perfect for Faster Productivity and as a scripting or glue language for integrating existing components. The readability of Python's succinct, easy-to-learn syntax is prioritized, lowering software maintenance costs. Python supports modules and packages, which encourages code reuse and software modularity. For all major systems, the Python interpreter and therefore its extensive standard library are available for free download and distribution in source or binary form.

Learning how to begin programming on a computer might seem to be a daunting task. There are several other programming alternatives available, but most of them are difficult to master, take chance to sort out, and don't always do what you need. Many individuals believe that in order to reach the level of coding that they want, they must be very intelligent or have extensive coding schooling and experience. Python, on the other hand, makes programming accessible to even the most inexperienced programmer. Python has enabled it really simple to get involved with coding, whether you're a complete novice or a seasoned pro. This language is based on English, so it's simple to read, and it's free of a lot of other symbols that render coding difficult for others to understand. Furthermore, since it is a user domain, anybody may make modifications and see other scripts to make things simpler. This handbook has spent a lot of time discussing the many functions available in Python as well as how simple it is to get started as a newbie. You will discover that this procedure is simple to learn and master with a little practice. It's simple to use, works on a number of platforms, and maybe even come pre-installed on newer Mac computers. Python is an excellent place to start whether you want to learn how to program or if you want to discover a software that can accomplish a lot of things without all of the fuss. It is among the most popular programming languages, and you'll find it simple to read and understand, especially if you have no clue where to begin.

Python is widespread among programmers because it allows them to work more efficiently. Python programs are easy to troubleshoot. A segmentation fault is never caused by a bug or faulty input. An inter preter throws an exception when it encounters an error. If the program fails to capture the error, the interpreter generates a trace of stack. Python was used to create the debugger, exhibiting Python's introspective capabilities.

www.ingramcontent.com/pod-product-compliance
Lightning Source LLC
Chambersburg PA
CBHW081807200326
41597CB00023B/4180